£350

BFI Film Cla

The BFI Film Classics is a series of books s, interprets and celebrates landmarks of world cinema. Each volume offers an argument for the film's 'classic' status, together with discussion of its production and reception history, its place within a genre or national cinema, an account of its technical and aesthetic importance, and in many cases, the author's personal response to the film.

For a full list of titles available in the series, please visit our website: www.palgrave.com/bfi

'Magnificently concentrated examples of flowing freeform critical poetry.'
Uncut

'A formidable body of work collectively generating some fascinating insights into the evolution of cinema.'
Times Higher Education Supplement

'The series is a landmark in film criticism.'
Quarterly Review of Film and Video

'Possibly the most bountiful book series in the history of film criticism.'
Jonathan Rosenbaum, *Film Comment*

To Tony + Tim with best wishes,

Doctor Zhivago

Ian Christie

[signature]

palgrave

A BFI book published by Palgrave

First published in 2015 by
PALGRAVE

on behalf of the

BRITISH FILM INSTITUTE
21 Stephen Street, London W1T 1LN
www.bfi.org.uk

There's more to discover about film and television through the BFI. Our world-renowned archive, cinemas, festivals, films, publications and learning resources are here to inspire you.

Palgrave in the UK is an imprint of Macmillan Publishers Limited, registered in England, company number 785998, of 4 Crinan Street, London N1 9XW. Palgrave Macmillan in the US is a division of St Martin's Press LLC, 175 Fifth Avenue, New York, NY 10010. Palgrave is a global imprint of the above companies and is represented throughout the world. Palgrave® and Macmillan® are registered trademarks in the United States, the United Kingdom, Europe and other countries.

Front cover design: Michał Janowski
Series text design: ketchup/SE14
Images from *Doctor Zhivago* (David Lean, 1965), © Metro-Goldwyn-Mayer; *Young Cassidy* (Jack Cardiff, 1965), © Sextant Films; *King and Country* (Joseph Losey, 1964), © B.H.E. Productions; *Great Expectations* (David Lean, 1946), Independent Producers; *War and Peace* (King Vidor, 1956), Ponti-De Laurentiis; *Doctor Zhivago* (Giacomo Campiotti, 2002), Granada/E-Vision/WGBH; *Star Wars: Episode II – Attack of the Clones* (George Lucas, 2002), © Lucasfilm Ltd/Twentieth Century-Fox Film Corporation; *Cathy Come Home* (Ken Loach, 1966), BBC.

Set by Cambrian Typesetters, Camberley, Surrey
Printed in China

This book is printed on paper suitable for recycling and made from fully managed and sustained forest sources. Logging, pulping and manufacturing processes are expected to conform to the environmental regulations of the country of origin.

British Library Cataloguing-in-Publication Data
A catalogue record for this book is available from the British Library
A catalog record for this book is available from the Library of Congress

ISBN 978–1–84457–921–1

Contents

Acknowledgments

This small book about a large film could not have been written without frequent reference to Kevin Brownlow's magnificent 1996 biography of David Lean, itself based on conversations with the director and with many of his associates, and on major collections of documents. It also draws upon my own research for *The Art of Film: John Box and Production Design* (2008), which was informed by extended conversations with its subject and a number of his colleagues, including Terence Marsh and Phyllis Dalton, both key to the making of *Zhivago*. The first, invaluable reader of my text was Patsy Nightingale, to whom all thanks for helping it and much else happen.

Particular thanks are due to Phyllis Dalton, Wim Jansen of Movie Ink Gallery, Amsterdam, and Andreï Kozovoï for permission to reproduce key photographs. Also to Sophia Contento and Philippa Hudson for making possible its rapid production with scrupulous attention to detail.

1 How *Zhivago* Happened

Several years ago, I was at a small garden party in North London, and gradually realised that I was sitting close to Julie Christie. What should I do? Pretend not to be aware of who she was, or launch into some appropriate conversation? Not wanting to embarrass the actress, I eventually said something about being fascinated by the colour design of *Doctor Zhivago*, after recently writing a book about its designer, John Box. Especially the blaze of yellow that lights up the library where Christie's character, Lara, is working when Zhivago rediscovers her after they have been separated by the Revolution. Immediately, Christie's face lit up at what seemed to be still a vivid memory, and I felt I had touched a chord that meant something to both of us, far beyond talk about the making of the film or its more obvious reputation. And indeed, that moment was a key image for the film's writer, Robert Bolt – who imagined 'an ocean of daffodils' for the scene that leads up to this fateful meeting – soon after he first agreed to write the script.[1]

I had come back to the film because of my association with the production designer John Box. Having committed to writing a book about his vision of the designer's role, I had to take on board the full range of films he had worked on, of which *Zhivago* was probably the best known, after *Lawrence of Arabia* (1962). And as with *Lawrence*, I was conscious of having to overcome the prejudices of youth. During the 1960s and 70s, when 'film studies' was still taking shape as a field of study, polemic played a vital role in defining the new subject. It was as important to declare what you were against in cinema as what you were championing. And David Lean's 'epics' *Lawrence* and *Zhivago* came high among the targets of cinephile contempt. During the years I spent arguing for Michael Powell and Emeric Pressburger's then little-known work, Lean also stood as a baleful comparison, with his seemingly overblown triumph, at a time when neither of his former mentors could get their own projects off the ground.

By the time I came to know John Box, I had developed a high regard for Lean's films of the 1940s and 50s, especially his skilfully modernised, and very English, family melodramas, from *This Happy Breed* (1944) to *The Passionate Friends* (1949). This was probably helped by film studies, now firmly established, having enthusiastically embraced melodrama, encouraged by its alliance with feminism during the 1970s, and arguing for films such as those of Douglas Sirk that had long been scorned as 'women's fiction'. Getting to know John Box led me to view and re-view not only the films he had designed for Lean, but also those that had influenced him, such as Lean's two Dickens adaptations, *Great Expectations* (1946) and *Oliver Twist* (1948), brilliantly conceived by one of his mentors, John Bryan. Coming back to *Zhivago*, I was seeing it through very different eyes.

Doctor Zhivago is of course many things. Despite an initial, and somewhat exaggerated, critics' drubbing, it became, as the late Omar Sharif says in his DVD introduction, 'an instant hit with romantics worldwide'. And for a vast audience, it still represents the epitome of modern romantic fiction, with the poet Zhivago and his beloved Lara ensconced in an ice-bound dacha, temporarily safe from the tides of revolution breaking around them. For others, it is a chronicle of disillusion with the Russian Revolution by the poet Pasternak, possibly overreaching himself in attempting the epic scale of Tolstoy's *War and Peace*. And for many, it stands as a monument, heroic or outdated depending on taste, to the heyday of the movie blockbuster, epitomised by the original MGM poster of its stars dwarfing the historical events that surround them. But it is unquestionably two material, historic things: a novel that became a worldwide best-seller and a political cause célèbre like no other in the mid-twentieth century; and a hugely popular film starring Julie Christie and Omar Sharif that won five Academy Awards in 1966, with theme music by Maurice Jarre that became inescapable for decades.

If the relationship between these has hardly been a subject of much critical attention, this is probably due to the assumption that a serious novel could not become a popular film without gross simplification or distortion. So is it worth trying to keep Pasternak's novel in view as we consider Lean's film? Up to a point I believe it is, although the novel should not be invoked to belittle the film, as we look back at two works that are now half a century old, both belonging to an era we struggle to recall, when books and films could shake the foundations of the cultural and political world.[2]

Boris Pasternak and the *Zhivago* storm

Perhaps the most famous anecdote about Boris Pasternak, the highly regarded poet who turned to prose for this solitary novel, concerns his only direct contact with Josef Stalin. In 1934, with Stalin's drive for conformity among artists in all media gaining momentum, the dictator telephoned the poet. Shortly before, a fellow Russian poet, Osip Mandelstam, had been arrested by the People's Commissariat for Internal Affairs (NKVD), and Pasternak tried to use his influence to get Mandelstam released. As a result, the phone rang in his apartment and 'Comrade Stalin' was announced. According to some accounts of what followed, Stalin asked, 'What are they saying in your circles about the arrest of Mandelstam?' Most, however, agree that Stalin assured Pasternak the poet's case had been reviewed and he would be safe, before the bizarre reproach: why hadn't Pasternak done anything to help Mandelstam? 'If I were a poet, and a poet friend was in trouble, I'd do anything to help him.' Pasternak would be haunted for the rest of his life by what happened next. His rambling answer apparently involved denying that there was any discussion of the case and explaining that 'friend' wasn't the right way to describe their relationship. According to some versions, Stalin insisted, 'But he's a genius', to which Pasternak replied that this wasn't the point; and in another account, Stalin accused Pasternak of 'not being able to stand up for a comrade'.[3]

Whatever the details, Pasternak was thunderstruck by this surreal conversation with a figure who fascinated him – and whose responsibility for Mandelstam's plight, among so many other arrests, was ignored. He told the story of the phone call endlessly, blaming himself in the terms that Stalin had blamed him, and so helping spread the rumour of Stalin's personal 'intervention' on behalf of Mandelstam. In fact, Mandelstam was rearrested in 1938 and died soon after in a prison camp during the Great Purge.
Pasternak, however, was never arrested, and his survival has been credited to Stalin's respect for his genius, and the note written against his name on an execution list, 'Do not touch this cloud-dweller.'

Immediately before and during the Second World War, Pasternak showed considerable courage, first refusing to sign a condemnation of senior officers during the Purge, despite strong pressure to do so; then making visits to troops to give poetry readings and boost morale. After the Allied victory, Stalin's paranoia led to wholesale imprisonment of returning veterans and renewed persecution of intellectuals. But Pasternak's own life took a new turn when the married writer met Olga Ivinskaya, a writer and young single mother, in October 1946 and fell in love with her. He had hoped to write a long novel for many years, probably since 1932 or even earlier; but inspired by his new love, he returned to what would become *Doctor Zhivago* and completed the manuscript in 1954. During this time, Ivinskaya paid a terrible price for her relationship with Pasternak, being arrested and imprisoned in 1949, and miscarrying their child in the process.

The novel now reflected their own story and aspirations, with Yuri Zhivago a married poet who falls in love with a nurse, Larissa (Lara), and, amid the chaos of the civil war, spends an idyllic few months at a remote dacha, before they finally separate and he returns to Moscow. The novel ends with a collection of poems attributed to Zhivago, which include many dedicated by Pasternak to Olga. But any hopes that it could be published in the Soviet Union, even during what became known as 'the Thaw' under Khrushchev's

leadership, were soon dashed when the editors of the journal that Pasternak submitted it to denounced the novel as 'anti-Soviet' and accused its author of being 'alienated' from his own society. Frustrated and disillusioned, Pasternak began to act recklessly, giving typescripts to different messengers to take abroad. One of these reached the Italian Communist publisher, Giangiacomo Feltrinelli, and the furious negotiation, not to mention anguish, that this created has only recently been revealed in Paolo Mancosu's aptly titled book *Inside the Zhivago Storm*.[4] But Feltrinelli was not the only interested party abroad. The CIA had also decided that the novel could be a major weapon in their propaganda war, and were actively trying to have it published in Russian and smuggled into the USSR.

Another recent book by Peter Finn and Petra Couvée has anatomised *The Zhivago Affair*, with its many players and spy-story twists (including smuggled rolls of microfilm involving Britain's MI6), which led to a special Russian-language edition being distributed at the Brussels International Exposition through the Vatican pavilion![5] Meanwhile, Feltrinelli's Italian edition of 1957 had been rapidly followed by translations into most main languages, and *Zhivago* becoming an international phenomenon. Despite some negative views, notably from the émigré Russian author Vladimir Nabokov, then enjoying English-language success with his novel *Lolita*, both critics and public seemed convinced that this marked 'one of the great events in man's literary and moral history', as the American critic Edmund Wilson hailed it.[6]

Boris Pasternak c. 1959, with Olga Ivinskaya and her daughter Irina: the relationship that inspired *Doctor Zhivago* and its story of a romantic passion that transcended the lives of those involved (courtesy of Andreï Kozovoï)

To cap it all, 1958 ended with the award of the Nobel Prize for Literature to Pasternak, linking *Zhivago* with the body of his earlier poetry and prose that had made him a contender for many years. The political storm in the Soviet Union was now intense. With the Cold War at its height, Pasternak was attacked from all sides, on Khrushchev's orders. Told that if he travelled to Stockholm he would be refused re-entry to Russia, Pasternak wrote to explain that he could not accept the award, creating even more anti-Soviet publicity in the process, and further increasing interest in *Zhivago*. Pasternak died two years later, his life probably shortened by the strain of surviving the Nobel Prize affair and the continued Soviet attacks on his integrity. Olga Ivinskaya was again arrested, on a trumped-up charge of currency speculation, although neither she nor Pasternak's wife ever benefited from the book's vast sales abroad. And although a later Soviet dissident, Alexander Solzhenitsyn, would criticise Pasternak for refusing the Nobel Prize, his very survival to continue writing and die a natural death set a historic example. Whether or not *Zhivago* ultimately measures up to either Tolstoy or Solzhenitsyn, it remains a literary landmark and the first modern Russian novel to enjoy an international impact.[7]

Starting the journey to the screen

The worldwide success of the novel virtually guaranteed that there would be strong interest in a film version. And because it effectively

Pasternak's Nobel citation was for his poetry and achievement 'in the field of the great Russian epic tradition' belonged to its Italian publisher, Feltrinelli, it was perhaps not surprising that the rights were secured by an Italian producer, Carlo Ponti. One of the longest-established figures in Italian cinema, Ponti was most identified with the career of his second wife, Sophia Loren, which had already led him to Hollywood. But he had also produced Fellini's breakthrough *La strada* (1954) and, more relevantly, executive-produced his one-time partner Dino De Laurentiis's epic *War and Peace* (1956), directed by Hollywood veteran King Vidor with an international cast, and based at Cinecittà Studios in Rome.

It seems that Ponti may have envisaged a similar production of *Zhivago*, with Loren taking the plum role of Lara, and a Hollywood major providing the finance, as Paramount had for *War and Peace*. In this case, it would be MGM who paid $450,000 for the worldwide rights, according to a memoir by Feltrinelli's son, which also claims that a draft contract listing potential directors amounted to a who's who of world cinema at the time: Fellini, Visconti, De Sica, David Lean, Carol Reed, Elia Kazan, Stanley Kubrick, Joseph Mankiewicz and, more improbably, Billy Wilder and Peter Ustinov. Ponti later insisted that he always had Lean in mind, but the invitation may have owed more to a change in top management at MGM. After a run of heavy losses, culminating in the troubled *Mutiny on the Bounty* (Lewis Milestone, 1962), the studio's new president, Robert O'Brien, a staunch admirer of Lean, wanted him to direct a major production that would restore their fortunes.

With the spectacular success of *Lawrence of Arabia*, taking seven Academy Awards in 1963 and achieving both critical and box-office success, Lean was in an exceptional position, but also uncertain about his next move. While relishing the success of *Lawrence*, he undertook to film a segment of the New Testament epic *The Greatest Story Ever Told* (1965), as a favour to the embattled director George Stevens, and also perhaps to savour the experience of being, even briefly, a 'Hollywood director' at one of the historic studios. With his personal life deeply conflicted by a growing rift with his fourth wife, he was looking for something that would satisfy his ambition and seize his imagination. There was apparently a wide range of mostly epic projects on offer, including the Joseph Conrad novel *Nostromo* (which would become Lean's last, unrealised project); Cecil Woodham-Smith's account of the Battle of Balaclava, *The Reason Why* (eventually filmed by Tony Richardson in 1968); John Buchan's *Prester John*; a Brazilian adventure yarn by James Ullman, *River of the Sun*; and James Mitchener's *Hawaii*. But *Lawrence* had engrossed him for so long that the risk of anticlimax seemed great.

Then, as Lean left Hollywood for the journey back to Europe, he was given *Doctor Zhivago* – an unenticing 500-plus pages for a slow reader. Yet by the time the liner *Leonardo da Vinci* docked, he was convinced, after being deeply moved by the book. Here was another epic he could believe in.

MGM, led by O'Brien, also believed in Lean as the director best suited to turn their expensive property into a successful blockbuster. They and Ponti were willing to agree to his terms, which involved a substantial payment up front and a share of profits, total freedom on the production, and his choice of screenwriter and crew. After the experience of Sam Spiegel's

interference on both *The Bridge on the River Kwai* (1957) and *Lawrence*, Lean was desperate to regain his independence; and he was equally keen to work again with Robert Bolt after the strong rapport they had developed on *Lawrence*. Bolt was immediately responsive to the project, despite his other commitments. So too was the production designer John Box, who, like Bolt, had joined *Lawrence*

Three of the chief architects of *Doctor Zhivago*: (from left to right) Carlo Ponti, Robert O'Brien and David Lean at the film's premiere (courtesy of Movie Ink. Amsterdam) when the project was in trouble, and forged a strong personal as well as professional relationship with Lean.

Straightening cobwebs: rewriting Zhivago

Doctor Zhivago is a substantial novel, conceived on the scale of Tolstoy, whom Pasternak's highly artistic family had actually known at the start of the century. Divided into sixteen multi-chapter parts with frequent chronological jumps, it covers an epic span of fifty years, and, perhaps hardest of all, its central characters never meet again after their passionate two months together, both dying before its end. To say the least, it presented formidable difficulties for the screenwriter. Lean, in fact, was no stranger to such problems of compression or selection. After his early association with the playwright Noël Coward, he had struck out independently with adaptations of Dickens's no less formidable novels, *Great Expectations* and *Oliver Twist*, for which he largely wrote the scripts, ruthlessly yet effectively reducing their complex criss-crossing storylines to manageable film plots. And faced with the problem of finding a structure for *Lawrence of Arabia*, a project that had baffled film-makers for decades, he discovered a kindred spirit in the playwright Robert Bolt, who had never written for the screen before.

A career schoolteacher with dramatic ambitions, Bolt's first plays were written for radio during the 1950s. Towards the end of the decade, he began to achieve professional stage production, culminating in his most famous play, *A Man for All Seasons* (1960), about Thomas More's conscientious refusal to accommodate Henry VIII. With highly successful productions running in London and New York, Bolt was launched as a major playwright, and no fewer than three television versions were broadcast before the Zinnemann film appeared in the year after *Zhivago*, winning even more Academy Awards. Unlike Lean, Bolt was deeply involved with the political and moral issues of the era. He had belonged to the British Communist Party and was active in anti-nuclear weapons campaigns, being arrested in 1961 as part of Bertrand Russell's Committee of 100, along with fellow playwrights John Arden, John Osborne and Arnold Wesker, when he was working on the *Lawrence* script.[8]

Once again, Lean felt sure that Bolt was the right choice for this new scripting challenge, with its unavoidably political dimension, and had insisted on this in his negotiations with Ponti and MGM. Although trying to return to his original vocation as a playwright, Bolt seemed more than happy to come on board: 'I am perfectly mesmerised by the idea of *Zhivago*. I love the book and it would be an honour to work on it with you.' But how to carve a script out of this sprawling narrative, even for a film of epic length?

We are fortunate to have an exchange of letters between Lean and Bolt, written while they were first grappling with this task.[9] Bolt seems to have started by assuming that the film would need to explain something of the complex history and political upheavals of Zhivago's lifespan, which runs from the last decade of tsarist Russia through the First World War and revolutions of 1917, and continues through Stalin's assumption of power in the mid-1920s and the terror of the following decade, into the Second World War and beyond. For Lean, however, it was above all a love story. 'We can't expect the mass audience to follow the refinement of conflict in [the political] area. It must be stated as simply as possible ... [while] the audience will understand every nuance of the love story.'[10]

Zhivago was not only a highly personal expression of love for Pasternak, but the film came at a significant time in their own lives for Lean and Bolt.[11] Both would separate from their wives during its making, and it is tempting to read the film as some kind of sublimation – the creation of a romantic ideal, when their own personal relationships had turned sour. Departing from Pasternak's essentially chronological novel, the basic structure of Bolt's screenplay would be very similar to that of *Lawrence*, using extended flashback to explore the central characters' lives from a point after their deaths. Yuri and Lara's origins and their meetings are evoked by Alex Guinness's Yevgraf, technically Yuri's half-brother, but in effect the film's narrator, as he uses his powerful rank in the Soviet security

apparatus to locate Lara's daughter by Yuri. This girl, unnamed in the film and played by another rising young star of the 1960s, Rita Tushingham, is the novel's Tanya, and the film becomes essentially the story of her parents.

Yevgraf's meeting with Tanya is located in a massive Soviet industrial plant that evokes the large-scale Ukrainian construction projects of the 1930s. But Bolt's screenplay quickly moves back to the novel's beginning in 1903, with a very young Yuri orphaned by the death of his mother in the Russian far east, and the complications of what befalls him during childhood and adolescence are efficiently condensed into his adoption by the wealthy Gromeko family, who have a large house in Moscow. Yuri is now a medical student, planning to devote his life to helping the sick rather than to research, while all around him political tension is rising. From the balcony of the Gromeko house, he witnesses the brutal suppression of a workers' demonstration by Cossack cavalry, in what became a deliberate avoidance of Eisenstein's famously detailed sequence of the civilian massacre in *The Battleship Potemkin* (1926).[12]

The major challenge of Bolt's work on the script was to eliminate the novel's many minor characters and digressions – 'retardations' in the language of Russian literary theorist Viktor Shklovsky – and to create a framework of dramatic logic for the

Stalin's name decorates the plant where the flashback, narrated by Yuri's half-brother Yevgraf (Alec Guinness), starts and ends central figures' meetings, often seemingly coincidental, and indeed their partings. At one point, before moving to Madrid to work directly with Lean, Bolt gave vent to his frustration: 'I've never done anything so *difficult*. That *bugger* Pasternak! It's like trying to straighten cobwebs.'[13] The metaphor seems particularly apt, since Pasternak was not a novelist by vocation, but a lyric poet, yet wanted above all to create a novel in the great tradition of Russian literature that grappled with historical events, while trying to evoke the inner life of its protagonists. Once Bolt accepted Lean's interpretation of what the film could be – a conflicted love story – then he was committed to trying to straighten Zhivago's complex relationships and juxtapositions.

If the turbulent historical background chronicled in the novel is one problem, another is the issue of Yuri as a poet. This was obviously central for Pasternak, as a highly regarded poet himself, but posed a major problem for the film-makers. Warming to his task, Bolt wrote to Lean that it seemed to be 'the old story of the woman falling not for the man but the artist, not realising that only the man and not the artist can return her love'.[14] This provoked a remarkable response from Lean, born of his own reflections on sexuality and creativity, which amounted to virtually a credo: 'isn't love-making one of the greatest forms of self-expression known to a man? (It certainly is to a woman.) ... Doesn't imagination, power, lyricism and the ability to disclose form the basis of both love and art?'[15] For Lean and Bolt, the film had become a surprisingly personal way of working through issues that they faced in their own lives – as the novel had been for Pasternak. When Bolt's wife left him while he was working on the script, both Lean and his mistress Barbara Cole felt that this coloured Bolt's approach to Lara, helping him make her a feminine ideal, as she also became for Lean, who was by then estranged from his wife Leila.

And there remained the central problem of how to achieve what Pasternak had done by appending twenty of his own poems as the 'evidence' of Zhivago's inspired creativity. Much of this is vested in Yuri and Lara's winter in the dacha at Varykino, which is the only

time in the film that we see him 'at work' as a poet.

Pasternak had Yuri admit that their flight was 'utter madness'; and Bolt agreed that it 'is in practical terms nonsense'. But thematically it had become vital, as he explained to an American journalist:

> We're hoping that the audience will now believe that this was a kind of *Tristan and Iseult* situation, a great, grand passion. And we have tried to arrange this sequence so that the climax of it shall be the writing of this poetry. In that way we hope to make poetry the crown of the film.[16]

After the strenuous final weeks of work on the script in Madrid, Bolt wrote of his gratitude for Lean's contribution, describing it as '"ours" not "mine"', and in particular his admiration for the director's 'flair and … detestation of the peripheral, the torpid and the hinted at'. The result, he predicted, 'may well be exceptional'.

Location, location: the view from the art department

But why Madrid? To understand the decision to base most of *Zhivago*'s filming in Spain involves realising how much Lean had come to depend not only on Robert Bolt but on the production designer of *Lawrence*, John Box. Box entered the film industry in 1948 after distinguished war service and training as an architect. Serving his apprenticeship in the art department at Denham Studios, in the last days of the British studio era, taught him the fundamentals, as well as the cost-saving tricks, of the profession. Seasoned designers such as John Bryan and Alex Vetchinsky, who were his mentors, had

As an admirer of the novel, Bolt hoped that Yuri's writing would form 'the crown of the film' when he and Lara escape to Varykino learned not to build more than was needed to create atmosphere on screen – and atmosphere was what Box valued above all.

He first worked in Spain on *The Black Knight* (Tay Garnett, 1954), an improbable Arthurian yarn starring Alan Ladd, made by Albert Broccoli and Irving Allen's Warwick Productions and based at Pinewood Studios, with locations in Wales as well as Spain. For the next four years, Warwick would offer Box a variety of challenges, usually to create exotic settings on a modest budget. The climax of this period of his career came with a Columbia A-list production, *The Inn of the Sixth Happiness* (Mark Robson, 1958), based on the early life of an English missionary to China, Gladys Aylward. Shooting on location in the China of Mao Tse-tung was impossible, so Box came up with the idea of using the landscape of North Wales, with suitable insertions of 'Chinese' architecture and detail.

Box's rising reputation for such resourcefulness undoubtedly recommended him as a suitable replacement for his one-time mentor John Bryan, who had fallen ill at the beginning of *Lawrence of Arabia*. When he arrived in the Jordanian desert, Box found Lean already well acclimatised, in fact so fascinated by the desert that he was reluctant to consider moving to the other settings that the film's script called for, and was adamantly opposed to working in a studio. So, while Box worked alongside Lean and cinematographer Freddie Young on the great desert scenes of *Lawrence*, he was also desperately searching for locations that would accommodate the remaining sequences set in Cairo, Damascus and Jerusalem. The solution turned out to be a variety of buildings in Spain's Seville, especially the elaborate 'Moorish' style of the Plaza de España, built for an unsuccessful Ibero-American Exposition world's fair in 1929, which became the Cairo officers' club (and has since been used for several *Star Wars* films). Other Moorish-themed Seville buildings stood in for Jerusalem and Damascus, while additional sets were built elsewhere in Spain, with Box and his team creating a pared-down version of the Red Sea port of Aqaba behind the beach of Playa del Algarrobico near Almeria, solely for the

spectacular attack on the Turkish garrison mounted by Lawrence
and his Bedouin forces.

During the long and complex filming of *Lawrence*, Lean had
learned to trust Box and felt confident that they shared a similar
approach to the importance of 'real' (though not necessarily
authentic) settings. But Spain was neither the immediate nor obvious
choice for filming *Zhivago*. Nor was Soviet Russia, despite an
invitation from the Soviet authorities to visit Moscow – not to offer
it as a location, but to explain why Lean shouldn't make a film of an
allegedly anti-Soviet novel at all. Carlo Ponti had hoped that Italy
would provide enough locations, and so Box's art director Terence
Marsh dutifully toured northern Italy, and especially the Dolomite
mountains, in the company of an aristocratic friend of Ponti's,
before reporting that Lean would not be satisfied by anything they
had seen.

Vast and snowy landscapes were by no means the only
requirement – any more than desert was for *Lawrence*.
Logistical feasibility was a high consideration for this scale of
production, and so was the atmosphere in which the actors and crew
would be working. For these reasons, several promising locations
were discounted. MGM suggested Canada, and Box inspected some
of its far north, which he found 'visually fascinating, but impossible
to film in' (although some snowy landscapes were shot in Alberta).
Apart from this, he was worried about 'the idiom being so American'
when they would be trying to create the sense of being in Russia.
Another reconnoitring trip seemed more promising, when Box and
Lean visited Yugoslavia, 'right on the doorstep of Russia' and
nominally a Communist country, although at this time following a
distinctly independent political line under Tito. Five years later,
Yugoslavia would provide many locations for another view of
Russia's tumultuous early twentieth-century history in *Nicholas and
Alexandra* (Franklin J. Schaffner, 1971), designed and partly directed
by John Box. But in both Box and Lean's accounts, their 1964
reception was anything but welcoming.

Finland, bordering on Russia and sharing its fierce climate, was
another possibility. Box and Lean drove north, and found 'marvellous
locations, on high ground overlooking Russia', which they decided
would be ideal for the winter sequence after Zhivago escapes from the
partisan unit that has forced him to become their doctor. But however
photogenic and atmospheric Finland might be, it remained
'logistically hopeless' for a big film that would require large-scale set
construction. The answer, of course, turned out once again to be
Spain, which could provide a range of locations suited to different
aspects of the story. Searching for somewhere to build the all-
important dacha at Varykino, Box and Marsh chose the remote
northern area of Soria, in Castilla y León, which could usually rely on
snow during the winter months and was served by a railway that had
steam trains. But their major find was in a suburb of Madrid, where a
new housing development was taking shape near the CEA Studios
that would be used for interiors. The production managed to reach an
agreement with the developer to use his building site, with an already

'Moscow in Madrid': Box's set burgeoned as a community during production and
provided a striking photo opportunity

paved central road, to build what soon became known as 'Moscow in Madrid'.[17] On this site, Box's art department would create an unusually substantial set that replicated aspects of the real Moscow on a reduced scale. The rising gradient of the main street was especially valuable, 'because you can use perspective to make it seem longer than it is',[18] as was the opportunity to borrow local historic trams for two crucial sequences that frame the narrative.

Above all, building a compact model Moscow, as he would later do for Dickensian London in *Oliver!* (Carol Reed, 1968), allowed Box to create the feel of a real city, with interconnecting streets and composite buildings. This meant that actors' entrances and exits could be followed, giving an unusual sense of spatial integrity to the vision of a city. When Lara gets off the tram she unwittingly shares with Yuri near the beginning, she moves through a street which takes her to Pasha, her zealous young lover, who is cautioned by police for distributing revolutionary leaflets. And in the same sequence, when Yuri enters the Gromekos' house, the camera follows him upstairs to reveal a view through the large salon window of buildings that evoke, rather than accurately represent, Moscow landmarks. Lean had grown to dislike intensely process photography, with back-projection and mattes extending the usually fragmentary built sets. And this solid yet schematic Moscow offered many more options to portray convincing journeys by characters than he had

A compact Moscow seen through the Gromekos' window helps 'anchor' the film in an imagined Russia

known back in the era of cramped studio-based filming. The scale of
the set is recorded in famous publicity pictures showing the actors
spread out across its 'main street', and many of those involved
remembered how it became a kind of virtual community during the
production. Roy Walker, assistant art director, was in charge of this
'little town', which soon boasted 'several tapas bars, a shoe repairer
and a knife sharpener, all with their signs up'.[19]

Casting and choosing locations

When Ponti had acquired the rights to *Zhivago*, he almost certainly
hoped that his wife Sophia Loren would star as Lara. However, Lean
realised that the role required not only a younger actress, but one
bringing fewer associations from past appearances. Lara is seen first
as an adolescent, seduced by her mother's overbearing lover, and then
as the young wife of the militant Antipov, before she and Yuri
Zhivago yield to their mutual passion. In some ways, the character

Julie Christie with Rod Taylor in *Young Cassidy* (1965), which clinched her casting
as Lara

echoes that of Natasha in *War and Peace*, as an ideal to whom different men are attracted, while Pasternak was strongly motivated in creating her by his new-found love for Ivinskaya. Trying to cast the central roles, Lean was bombarded with suggestions from many sides, mostly of established stars. But the choice of Julie Christie, just twenty-four at the time, came after Lean saw her as the free spirit who tantalises young Billy in John Schlesinger's *Billy Liar* (1963) and, improbably, from consulting the veteran John Ford. Ford had started directing *Young Cassidy* (1965), based on the autobiography of Sean O'Casey, with Christie making only her second film appearance as an early girlfriend, before illness forced him to hand over the film to Jack Cardiff. But when Lean asked about the young actress, Ford was apparently fulsome in his praise. Christie had already filmed Schlesinger's *Darling* (to be released in mid-1965) and was becoming recognised as a contemporary icon when she was invited to Madrid, where Lean was quickly convinced that she combined the innocence and allure of Lara.

Casting the name part of the poet Yuri Zhivago proved more straightforward. After Paul Newman, Burt Lancaster and Max von Sydow had all been rejected, Lean wanted Peter O'Toole, as if he were trying to reassemble the happy band that had made *Lawrence*. O'Toole, however, was under contract to Sam Spiegel, who was certainly not going to assist Lean's disloyalty to him. It also appears that, after seeing a script, O'Toole was not happy about the part. So Lean followed the suggestion of his closest associate, Barbara Cole, and invited the other *Lawrence* newcomer Omar Sharif to play this difficult role of a largely passive 'good man'.

The other figures in Lara's life are her mother's lover and lawyer Komarovsky and the idealistic young student Pasha Antipov, two men who negotiate the Bolshevik revolution in very different ways. For Komarovsky, described by Lean as 'a man of the flesh … and its desires; food, comfort and sex', the director's first choice was Marlon Brando, who however failed to respond to the invitation. His second was James Mason, the veteran British leading man who had recently

enjoyed a major success as the lover of the nymphet in *Lolita* (Stanley Kubrick, 1962). Mason apparently accepted with alacrity, but the part went instead to the reliably cynical Rod Steiger, who was proud to find himself the only American in the cast. For Lara's first husband and later her nemesis, Lean turned to one of the rising generation of British actors associated with 'Northern realism', Tom Courtenay, who was Christie's co-star in *Billy Liar*. Perhaps more significantly, Courtenay had recently played a hapless young First World War soldier who deserts on the Western Front and is court-martialled, in Joseph Losey's *King and Country* (1964), for which he won the Best Actor award at the Venice Film Festival that year, shortly before *Zhivago* started shooting.[20]

Both Yuri and Lara are already married when they fall in love, and for the part of Zhivago's wife, with whom he has two children, Lean had apparently hoped for Audrey Hepburn, perhaps remembering her Natasha from Vidor's *War and Peace*. It was Carlo Ponti who urged him to consider the inexperienced Geraldine Chaplin, the twenty-year-old daughter of Charles and Oona Chaplin. After her screen test, he was as persuaded as he had been of Christie. The Gromekos, Yuri's foster-family following the death of his parents, were played by the veteran Ralph Richardson, star of an earlier Lean triumph, *The Sound Barrier* (1952), and the Irish actress Siobhan McKenna.

Omar Sharif had to undergo severe make-up transformation to appear 'Russian'

But Lean had some difficulty in persuading another of his old colleagues to accept the role of a narrator that Bolt had created in his adaptation. Yuri's half-brother has become a general in the NKVD, and plays little part in Yuri's life until, after his death, Lara persuades him to help her search for her abandoned daughter. In Bolt's dramatisation, Yevgraf becomes the narrator of this simplified, yet still complex story. But when Lean asked Alec Guinness to play the role, he had to work hard to persuade the actor that this would amount to more than being a mere commentator. The two had first worked together at the start of their careers, with Guinness starring in both of Lean's Dickens adaptations, *Great Expectations* and *Oliver Twist*. But despite their recent triumphs together in *The Bridge on the River Kwai* (which had brought Guinness an Oscar) and *Lawrence*, their relationship was wary, even strained. Kevin Brownlow quotes the

Tom Courtenay (centre) as the hapless Private Hamp in Joseph Losey's *King and Country* (1964), a part prefiguring his role as the innocently idealistic Pasha in *Zhivago* exchanges between them that led to Guinness accepting the role, with reservations about the narration, after what he described as his 'initial shillyshallying'.[21]

Assembling the team

A number of other *Lawrence* stalwarts would return to join Lean on *Zhivago*: notably the costume designer Phyllis Dalton, director of photography Freddie Young and composer Maurice Jarre. In the interval, both Dalton and Young had worked on Richard Brooks's *Lord Jim* (1965), starring O'Toole, but were happy to answer the call to Madrid. Much of Dalton's contribution to *Lawrence* had been almost invisible to the audience, even though it involved costuming a vast number of Jordanian extras as traditional Bedouin, in varying stages of battle-weariness – with the masterstroke of dressing O'Toole in ever-thinner versions of his white robes, to suggest his growing fragility. But the costuming of *Zhivago* would involve a picturesque panoply of all things Russian, from the opulence of the

Costume designer Phyllis Dalton, with Tom Courtenay (courtesy of Phyllis Dalton)

tsarist period to the many uniforms and civilians' rags of the post-revolutionary era, finishing with the drab conformity of the Soviet 1930s.

Dalton was helped by a new member of the team, Andrew Mollo, who came from an Anglo-Russian family with a strong interest in the history of uniforms (his older brother John would become a highly regarded costume designer, starting with George Lucas's original *Star Wars* in 1977). Mollo was engaged to advise on the costuming and weaponry of the various military units that appear in the film, and his film-making partner Kevin Brownlow drew on his friend's experience to convey the tension that existed on set. Everyone was afraid of criticising or disappointing Lean, but for a historical period so rarely portrayed on screen, there was very little accurate information to hand. Mollo took a dim view of how the partisans who capture Zhivago were initially presented, 'looking like extras from *Taras Bulba*'.[22] But Lean proved attentive to his expertise, and soon they were provided with uniforms and the swords that Mollo knew they would have had in the civil war period. Having expected to work only a few weeks on the film, he eventually stayed for fifteen months – no doubt adding to the spiralling budget – yet was flabbergasted to receive no screen credit.

Young had won an Academy Award for the 70mm cinematography of *Lawrence*, but was not Lean's first choice for the new film. This was Nicolas Roeg, who had been second unit cameraman on *Lawrence* and indeed trained by Young. While Lean may have felt he wanted a younger and more daring director of photography, once the film was under way, there were frequent disagreements between the two, with the imperious Lean disliking Roeg's manner and finding some of his effects too daring in their use of very low light. An early idea had been to make the film in black and white and on 70mm, but when budget considerations ruled these out, Lean was encouraged by John Box to restrict the colour palette. One of the early scenes to be filmed was the big night-time demonstration in the Moscow main street, where the dark figures of

the demonstrators and the snow underfoot would be stained red
by the Cossacks' violent attack. There are different accounts of
what went wrong. According to Brownlow, Roeg mocked Lean's
call for more light on the scene as wanting it 'Hollywood';[23] while
Lean's favoured props and effects man, Eddie Fowlie, remembered
Roeg having difficulty lighting this large expanse, and then
effectively cancelling his fresh snow effect by turning on
foreground lights.[24] Fowlie recalled how Lean was frustrated by
the potential waste of a night's shooting, and hissed: 'That's it.
I'm going to have to let him go.' In the event, without any
explanation to the rest of the crew, Roeg departed and was quickly
replaced by Young, who would describe *Zhivago* in his own
memoir as 'the most memorable and challenging of all the pictures
I've worked on'.[25]

Young's immensely varied career stretched back to the silent
era, and both he and Lean had worked on the early wartime
propaganda film by Powell and Pressburger, *49th Parallel* (1941).
But capturing the range of *Zhivago*, from its epic scale to the extreme

Filming this set-piece apparently provoked Lean to sack Nicolas Roeg and bring in
Freddie Young as director of photography

intimacy of its central love story, and all in a very different climate and setting from the on-screen world the audience must believe in, would test Young's ingenuity. It also prompted him to revive old techniques such as vignetting, used when Yuri reaches Lara's house at Yuryatin. Vignetting was commonly employed in the silent era, to emphasis a star's signature image or disguise signs of age, and was achieved by 'stretching a piece of white gauze … a few inches in front of the lens, then using a lighted cigarette to burn a hole in the centre'. In *Zhivago*, its use is dramatic. Yuri has been 'wandering around in the snow for days [and] he looks in the mirror and this blotched, haggard face stares back at him':

We framed Omar's head in the hole in the gauze, then flooded the gauze with light from the front, taking care not to hit the lens. The result is everything appears white except Omar's face. The viewer's attention is concentrated on the face, and they share the character's horrified reaction to his own appearance.[26]

Young clearly found the film's 'enormous variety of mood and situation' challenging, but also stimulating, as did all the key production personnel.

Discussing the intensive and arduous production of *Zhivago* would be impossible without reference to Eddie Fowlie, who had become indispensable to Lean since working on *The Bridge on the River Kwai*. Although Fowlie is credited as 'property master' on *Lawrence* and for 'special effects' on *Zhivago*, and not at all on *Kwai*, he was responsible for some of the most memorable images in all these films – including the actual demolition of the bridge in *Kwai*. Fowlie's clumsy but accurate title for his autobiography, *David Lean's Dedicated Maniac: Memoirs of a Film Specialist*, refers to Lean's own description of his close team as 'dedicated maniacs', and none was more dedicated than Fowlie, who eventually became a close friend. Understanding Lean's character, as a perfectionist who also found communication difficult, Fowlie set out to fulfil the director's vision as completely as possible – sometimes to the point of interfering with the work of others on the crew.

John Box, whose art department overlapped with Fowlie's province, claimed they had had good relations, and some of the most widely admired images in *Zhivago* were the result of their collaboration. The interior of the Varykino 'ice palace' is certainly the most famous for which they shared credit. But there were other, subtle effects that Fowlie was able to introduce, such as 'putting two tiny pieces of glitter on the [balalaika] strings to enhance Freddie Young's lighting' for the childhood scene with Yuri, or the more complex effect of a candle melting condensation on the window for an emotional scene between Lara and her fiancé Pasha that was shot in a single take. Other ingenious effects conjured up by Fowlie 'never got beyond the cutting room floor', but his reward came at the end, when MGM asked how he would like to be credited, and offered 'special effects'. 'The whole of *Doctor Zhivago* was a special effect,' he concluded, 'but nobody saw it as such. That was my reward.'[27]

The composer is usually the last creative contributor to be contracted for a film, and is in the unenviable position of being unable to start work until the film's edit is finalised. A film score, which may become its major signature presence in the world, is surprisingly often treated as a mere afterthought. Maurice Jarre had first entered Lean's world due to a series of accidents, when Malcolm Arnold, who had written the score for *The Bridge on the River Kwai*, and William Walton, the veteran heavyweights of British composition, both turned down *Lawrence of Arabia* as 'terrible [and] needing hours of music'. But Sam Spiegel had heard Jarre's score for the French film *Sundays and Cybele/Les Dimanches de Ville d'Avray* (Serge Bourguignon, 1962), which won the 1963 Best Foreign Language Film Oscar, and so Jarre, who had mainly composed for documentaries and for art films such as those of Georges Franju, was abruptly promoted from creating links between the music of famous composers to writing and recording the entire score in six weeks.[28]

Despite the wide acclaim for his *Lawrence* score, capped by an Oscar and other awards, there was some dissent from MGM about Jarre being chosen for *Zhivago*.[29] But Lean was adamant, and Jarre was contracted in time to visit the production in Spain and begin to assimilate its atmosphere. Like *Lawrence*, this was to be a 'roadshow' presentation, complete with its overture and intermission, and the music would play an important part in establishing the sense of being in Russia.

But which Russia? The scenario reached from the tsarist era to Stalin's Soviet Union, mostly tracing the lives of those who had suffered during this violent upheaval. To evoke aspects of 'eternal Russia', in Moscow and in the distant countryside beyond the Urals, as well as of the Revolution and the Soviet era – all skilfully contrived outside Russia – the music would play a vital role, as it had done in all Lean's films. There was no shortage of Russian-born composers in

Maurice Jarre with Lean during their first collaboration, on *Lawrence of Arabia*; Lean took a keen interest in the music for his films, closely supervising the edit and mix

Hollywood, as MGM reminded the director, but he had been playing records of traditional Russian music on set to help create a Russian atmosphere for himself and the actors. And so, like the zither on the soundtrack of Carol Reed's *The Third Man* (1949), the balalaika would become the distinctive audible and visual motif of *Zhivago*. And indeed its cultural adaptability would help bridge the vast span of the film's narrative. First used in the eighteenth century and developed during the next hundred years, this three-stringed triangular instrument had achieved 'artistic' as well as folk status by the turn of the twentieth century. It was then enthusiastically promoted as both proletarian and distinctively Russian during the Soviet era, with a balalaika 'orchestra', using all seven versions of the instrument, eventually accompanying the popular Red Army choral and dance ensemble tours. Unusually, the instrument has also held its popularity among émigré communities, which would ease the task of recording Jarre's balalaika-heavy score in Los Angeles.

The balalaika would provide a distinctive musical motif and help bolster the film's Russianness

2 Between Beauty and Goodness: The Making of *Zhivago*[30]

Framing the *Zhivago* story

Pasternak's novel begins with a complex evocation of the early experiences of young Yuri Zhivago after his mother has died, as he is shuttled between relatives, not knowing the truth about his profligate father. The book also conveys a sense of the scale of Russia and of the slow tempo of life at the beginning of the twentieth century, reminiscent of Turgenev and Chekhov. Faced with the problem of how to engage a mass cinema audience in this unfamiliar world, Robert Bolt boldly introduced a framing story that is set in a somewhat generic though impressive version of the Soviet era, with an opening shot that pans up the boots and uniform of a stern military figure. This cuts to the image of a brightly lit tunnel in a sheer rock face, with an access bridge and a red star above the entrance. It's a shot that distantly evokes the first appearance of the shuffling lines of underground workers in Fritz Lang's *Metropolis* (1927), an early vision of a ruthlessly regimented future society. But Bolt quickly locates this scene during the massive industrial projects that had begun in the 1930s, as a manager complains to the uniformed officer that humans shouldn't be used to move earth.[31] The older man identifies himself as Yuri Zhivago's half-brother, clearly a senior Party figure, who is searching for his niece, the daughter of the dead poet and Lara, among the mass of workers; and a terse exchange between the two establishes that the writer's 'Lara' poems are enjoying great popularity – now that they can be read.

Considering the scandal that had surrounded Pasternak's novel, when it was published abroad while banned in the USSR, this was a highly effective way of acknowledging – and simplifying – the context for the story of Yuri Zhivago and his great love. Alec Guinness's character, Yevgraf, embodies all that western audiences were likely to assume about ruthless Soviet commissars, yet he is also allowed to voice the argument that hardship was inevitable in the early stages of building a new society: 'Don't be too impatient, Comrade Engineer; we've come very far, very fast ... But do you know what it cost? Children in those days who lived off human flesh – did you know that?' The images that follow show the same stream of workers, but increasingly as a crowd of individuals, looking far from regimented. Whatever position the film will take on the course of the Bolshevik revolution and Stalin's Soviet Union, it will not be simple condemnation. These workers crossing the head of a massive dam could belong to almost any industrial workforce, and seem much closer to the 1960s than the 30s. The *Zhivago* scandal had been followed by a key moment in Khrushchev's cultural 'Thaw': the permitted publication of Solzhenitsyn's *One Day in the Life of Ivan Denisovich* in 1962, which revealed the harsh world of the gulag labour camps to readers within the USSR and soon around the world. Bolt and Lean's *Zhivago* effectively announces itself as a western counterpart of the Thaw, ready to acknowledge past barbarity from a more humane present, despite its apparent location at what was the height of Stalin's terror.

A girl presents herself at the office door and enters warily. Rita Tushingham is identified only as 'the girl' and was, like Julie

The general explains to 'the girl' that her father 'lost his mother at about the same age as when your mother lost you'

Christie, a distinctly contemporary figure, a star of the early 1960s 'new wave' in British cinema. Her debut in *A Taste of Honey* (Tony Richardson, 1961) established a waif-like ingénue image that continued through her early roles; and this allows her to blankly parry the leading questions of General Zhivago, as he formally introduces himself and explains brusquely that he is looking for his niece. What follows is a somewhat contrived dialogue, which makes much use of an improbable illustrated edition of the Lara poems, with photographs of both Sharif and Christie conveniently establishing the central figures in the story to come. The bridge into that world – the structural equivalent of Lawrence being given his mission to enter the desert – is Yevgraf's line, 'He lost his mother at about the same age as when your mother lost you,' heard over Tushingham's purposely impassive face. Then a pause before he adds, '… and in the same part of the world', which cues a cut to a vast plain, backed by snow-capped mountains – a parallel to the breathtaking first vista of the desert in *Lawrence*. Here, however, the image is more structured. A Russian cross occupies the right side of the frame, and a small group of figures is moving from the distance on the left, with Russian church singing audible. An abrupt cut to the young Yuri carrying a bouquet reveals that it is a funeral procession: that of his mother.

However diagrammatic the general structure and dialogue of this scene, it is hard not to admire its economy and efficiency in

A dramatic cut transports us from the frame story's industrial setting to the Russian steppe, recalling the breathtaking first appearance of the desert in *Lawrence of Arabia*

preparing viewers for a narrative that had already been widely criticised for its mass of characters and sprawling chronology.

What follows is even more effective, and shows how the film will condense Pasternak's romantic vision into a series of concise and powerfully poetic images. Young Yuri is in bed, being welcomed by his new family, the Gromekos, who give him a balalaika that belonged to his mother. Will he have a gift as she did? Alexander Gromeko wonders. A little girl watches him silently; this is the Gromekos' daughter Tonya, who will later become his wife. And so his whole future is mapped out in this opening scene. But when he is left alone, first the balalaika theme associated with his mother is heard over a close-up of the instrument that is all he has of her. Then, in the next shot, the wind rises, blowing a wreath from the grave, which is gradually covered by a snowstorm – an echo perhaps of the powerful graveyard scene that opened Lean's first masterpiece, *Great Expectations*, twenty years earlier. But here, disturbed by the sound of a branch beating on the windowpane, young Yuri goes to the window and peers out, a frosted ring surrounding his face, as if looking towards his future.

This motif – of seeing something 'through a glass icily' – will recur throughout the film and seems to have had its origins in the reconnoitring trip to Finland by director and designer. John Box became intrigued by lakes freezing over and began to photograph them. This led to Lean buying Box an expensive Hasselblad camera

The recurring image of the frosted window stemmed from Box and Lean's recce to Finland

like his own, but more importantly the image of ice freezing suggested to Box a visual metaphor for the insistent 'pulsation of life' as a central theme of Pasternak's story. The first time we see it is when the young Yuri is looking towards an uncertain future; then the cut that follows – with ex-editor Lean's typical boldness – is to a vividly coloured microscope image that fills the screen. This leap in time and space takes us to Yuri as a medical student in Moscow, where he affirms to his professor that it is 'life' that beckons him rather than research. In the novel, Yuri becomes an expert in the physiology of sight, which connects with his interest in 'the imagery of art'; but perhaps more directly, Pasternak's most admired book of poetry had been called *My Sister, Life*.[32]

The brief scene in the laboratory that introduces Omar Sharif as the adult Yuri also shows the value of the Madrid set, with a window revealing the city bustle outside and a tram, which will soon serve to stage the first coincidental meeting between Yuri and Lara. Yuri runs to catch the tram, where Julie Christie is already a passenger, fur covering much of her face apart from her intense blue eyes. Yuri sits behind her, and both turn to look out of the window, as if in some way already linked. When Lara rises to get off, Yuri's glance lingers on her – and their future destiny together is cheekily predicted with a cut to the spark ignited by the tram's electrical arm. Again, the integrated set proves its value, as Lara hurries down a side street,

Yuri and Lara's first near-meeting, as they both travel in a Moscow tram, unaware of their linked future destiny

where she will meet her young fiancé, Pasha, in what appears to be a poorer district. The world of pre-revolutionary Russia is compressed into a manageable neighbourhood, where we quickly begin to find our bearings. No matter that the scale is vastly smaller than the real city, which few of the film's original audiences would have known at first hand; this miniaturised 'Moscow in Madrid' becomes a picturesque site of romantic coincidence, like a fully realised version of the Hollywood-built imaginary Vienna of Max Ophuls's *Letter from an Unknown Woman* (1948).

The colours of seduction and revolution

The film has economically introduced Lara and the two young men in her life within minutes. But the third, who will play a catalytic role, is neither young nor idealistic. Viktor Komarovsky was envisaged by Lean as 'a man of the flesh', and Rod Steiger establishes his sensuality from the outset in what is surely one of the film's very best performances. As the 'protector' and lover of Lara's mother, Amelia, he moves through her dressmaking workshop with a proprietorial air, and sizes up the seventeen-year-old Lara with evident relish, draping a scarf around her head and shoulders with a gesture of sexual possessiveness – as if testing whether she is ready to receive his closer attentions. Lara's mother also seems to collude in offering her daughter, possibly as a way to keep Komarovsky's

A sensual Komarovsky pointedly sizes up the young Lara in her mother's dressmaking workshop, as if preparing to transfer his amorous interest

waning interest. When she is too ill to accompany him to dinner, she urges him to take Lara instead. And so Lara makes her entry into the luxurious decadence of pre-revolutionary Moscow society, as an ingénue accompanying the well-known figure of Komarovsky.

The restaurant decor is entirely red and black with nude female statues in gold, its clientele wearing formal black and white, while Lara stands apart in a demure grey dress which amply covers her shoulders. The bold colour design of this and the scenes that follow shows how successfully the production co-ordinated art direction and costume design to depict personal lives caught up in the deepening crisis of tsarist Russia. Like the orchestration of a tone poem, with several themes running together, we move from the restaurant to a street demonstration, which is predominantly black against white snow, with the red of banners bearing the slogan 'Freedom and Brotherhood'. When the demonstrators are heard singing, back in the restaurant, Komarovsky jokes to the company that 'perhaps they will sing in tune after the Revolution'. Then, as he and Lara drive back from the restaurant in a sleigh, he forces himself upon her and his violence is intercut with a company of mounted troops waiting to attack the demonstrators. Pasha is prominent among the demonstrators, vigorously 'conducting' the band that accompanies them – an eerie echo of Courtenay's recent fantasy role in *Billy Liar*, as the ruler of the make-believe kingdom of Ambrosia.

Blood-splashed snow, represents the rising tide of protest that will lead to revolution

When the troops charge, their impact is conveyed through a staccato series of detail shots – a bewildered child, scattered band instruments, a red banner briefly filling the screen and, finally, a vivid splash of blood against the snow. Yuri is on the balcony of the Gromeko mansion, watching helplessly, but rushes to aid the injured before he is ordered by officers to go inside. Lara wanders through her mother's workshop, shaken by Komarovsky's assault, and sees her image in a mirror, wearing the same scarf that he draped around her at their first meeting. Soon her reverie is interrupted by the distorted image of Pasha seen through a glass door. When he enters, she recoils from the scar on the side of his head, and watches horrified as he pours iodine down his cheek from a blue bottle and faints from its burn, after asking her to hide his gun. This she does and also conceals Pasha when her mother appears, ghost-like in a pale green robe, and comments on her lateness, asking whether she is going to church. In the brief church scene, Lara receives terse counselling from a priest, who recalls the parable of the woman taken in adultery.

For a second time we now see Komarovsky confidently entering one of the luxurious settings that are his natural haunt. However, this is not a restaurant but a place of assignation, with more overtly sexual statue busts lining its curving gallery of doors leading to private rooms. Lara has been kept waiting for an hour in one of these, and now she is wearing a low-cut red dress. The colour of the dress had been a matter of negotiation among the film's makers. Phyllis Dalton initially designed it in black velvet, reasoning that this was what a young girl would choose for such an important occasion.[33] But Robert Bolt and Lean, described by Dalton as 'primitive British men', wanted it to be red. Dalton's technique for dealing with Lean's habitual indecisiveness was to produce costumes in different colours, and he chose the red, even though Julie Christie 'hated the colour' and felt anxious about playing the scene in the dress. In a sense, the symbolism of wearing a red dress at such an assignation, and especially after reference to the biblical parable of the adulteress, was all too obvious. But John Box's argument to

Christie was strategic: 'red's not your colour, so you'll play the scene perfectly because you'll be uncomfortable'. After the bloody splash of the massacre, the jarring red of Lara's dress serves to link her with the theme of growing violence, as a victim of autocratic power in the shape of Komarovsky.

Lara does indeed appear uncomfortable, as he taunts her and pours wine into her mouth, rubbing his hands across her wet lips and chin in a gesture that intensifies his earlier touching. A line of dialogue confirms that he has chosen the dress on her behalf, but the most perverse aspect of the scene is his insistence that Lara's mother knows what they are doing. He seems determined to break Lara's resistance by making her acknowledge this and calling her a hypocrite. Yet an aspect of Komarovsky's character in both novel and film is that, however venal his behaviour may be, there is some attraction between them. Here, he insists 'you'll always come back' as she flees the scene.

The transition that follows picks up the theme of Komarovsky's taunt, as the camera drifts across an exterior with snow falling and cranes up to show a bedroom window, through which a figure can be seen writhing on the bed. Komarovsky, now in shirtsleeves, is watching anxiously and quickly writes a note which he gives to a sleigh-driver in the street. The driver is to find a Professor Kurt at all costs and bring him to help. We cut to a soirée at the Gromekos',

A scarlet woman: the colour choreography of Lara's seduction by Komarovsky where Yuri's mentor and his wife are attending a concert in the great salon. But as the pianist starts to play Rachmaninov, the bored professor leaves his seat, and finds Yuri and Tonya sitting on the stairs engrossed in what is clearly a romantic conversation. The banter between the three is interrupted by the sleigh-driver delivering what we know must be Komarovsky's note, and, as if by fate, Yuri finds himself accompanying the professor to 'see some general practice' at first hand. When they arrive, it becomes clear that Amelia has poisoned herself on account of Komarovsky – and by drinking from the same luridly blue bottle of iodine that Pasha had used to cauterise his wound, now seen in full-screen close-up. As the professor prepares to pump her stomach, Amelia calls out Lara's name twice, while Yuri wanders into the semi-darkness of the workshop, and the premonitory four notes of the 'Lara' theme are heard. Yuri glimpses himself darkly mirrored in a window, suggestively echoing the childhood image of him at the frosted window; then in an eerie reflection image, he sees a woman's isolated arm and hand, before a light is switched on to reveal Lara asleep in a chair and Komarovsky entering.

Just how carefully planned was this disclosure of Lara to Yuri is revealed in Freddie Young's memoir, where he describes it as one of the 'touches [I'm] quite proud of'.[34] He also quotes a letter from Lean, clearly treasured, which provides a rare insight into the director's

'An almost black screen and a lighted hand ... Magic': Lean admired Freddie Young's lighting for Yuri's first sight of Lara

attitude to teamwork and to shaping the story visually: 'An almost black screen and a lighted hand. It was your idea completely. Very daring. Not realistic. Magic. Sensual delight.'[35] Lara and Komarovsky embrace, then Komarovsky's eyes meet those of Zhivago, before both make their way back to the bedroom where Amelia is being tended. In fact, reflections, repetitions and images distorted through multiple layers of glass recur throughout the film, creating visual links between the characters and arguably forming an equivalent to the 'cobwebs' of the novel that Bolt had struggled to straighten in his screenplay, while Lean translates them into visual relations.

This densely plotted passage illustrates Bolt and Lean's poetic compression of the novel, and how it aims to create a sense of proximity and synchronicity among the film's characters, even before they know each other. With virtually no transition shots or overviews, the gathering momentum of 'the Revolution' is compressed into a single demonstration and its brutal suppression, which in turn counterpoints the attempted seduction of Lara by Komarovsky, provoking her mother's suicide attempt, and also drawing Yuri into their orbit when he attends Lara's mother with his mentor and sees Lara with Komarovsky. Both Lara and Yuri are in effect 'present' as bystanders at the demonstration that encapsulates the growing agitation for profound change in Russia, much as Eisenstein had condensed the 1905 Revolution into his invented scene of the Odessa Steps massacre in *The Battleship Potemkin*.

Meanwhile, in a parallel world, Tonya returns from visiting Paris, fashionably yet frivolously dressed in pink, and is met at the station by Yuri and her parents, who fondly watch the growing closeness of the pair. Rather clumsily, we are reminded of Yuri's otherwise invisible status as a promising young poet when Tonya brandishes a French newspaper and tells him that he leads a survey of the Russian poetry scene. Lara and Tonya are established as contrasting poles of Yuri's affection. Tonya seems innocent, with a privileged life that will lead her naturally to marriage with Yuri and a proper respect for his idealism and poetic gift. But it is Lara who is

the dramatic focus of our attention, coping with the demands of both Komarovsky and Pasha, and emerging in the process as a young woman who has already known subjugation and suffering.

Her suffering reaches its climax when Komarovsky appears at the dressmaking workshop, his entrance announced by the 'filtered' image of the glass doors. Clearly frustrated by Lara's earlier resistance, he calls her a 'slut' and bears down on her in what appears to be a violent assault, during which her face is partly veiled by another scarf.[36] As Komarovsky contemptuously leaves, insisting that it was no rape for either of them, he is seen disappearing through the glass doors that shade characters' entrances and exits in this shabby art nouveau style antechamber to the decadent world that he inhabits. Humiliated, Lara resolves to take her revenge, and the pistol that Pasha had found during the revolutionary demonstration gives her the means to do so.

The third and last of the high society scenes finally brings together all the key characters who have now been introduced. Whether a Russian party in 1913 would have been quite so like a typical British or American Christmas gathering, with a large decorated tree, is doubtful. But the intention is to create a recognisable end-of-year celebration, which will also mark the end of the world that these privileged Russians inhabit. The party's hostess brings Yuri and Tonya together and announces their engagement. Meanwhile, Komarovsky is playing cards with his cronies in a corner.

Phyllis Dalton's design for the stylish pink dress that Tonya wears for her return from Paris (courtesy of Phyllis Dalton)

But we have been alerted to Lara's intention by intercut shots of her hurrying through the streets, followed at a distance by Pasha. As the party applauds the engagement, Lara advances on Komarovsky and clumsily shoots him. In the shocked silence, he freezes before sitting down heavily, seemingly not seriously wounded. Lara also freezes, unsure what to do next; but it is Pasha who strides through the paralysed revellers and steers her towards the door.
Komarovsky angrily rejects calling the police, wanting to minimise the scandal that Lara's act of revenge may bring.

A dissolve leads from the babble that follows to a lavatory, where Yuri is dressing Komarovsky's wounded arm. The parallel with their earlier meeting at Amelia's bedside is clear and perhaps overemphatic, but the motif of the scene is that their 'destinies are interwoven'.[37] Komarovsky quickly explains that he was more than Yuri's father's business partner and that he knows his half-brother, Yevgraf. He makes clear his pragmatism: the Bolsheviks can be respected as men, even if their programme is abhorrent, 'and they may win'. Yuri shyly confesses that he too is in contact with Yevgraf, 'and he likes my poetry'. The conversation takes a new turn as Komarovsky prepares to leave. Having assured Yuri that his father was 'not a bad man' and was devoted to his mother, this supremely confident figure seeks the same reassurance as before: 'I may continue to rely on your professional discretion?' But Yuri's thoughts and emotions are elsewhere. His eyes

The party announcing Yuri and Tonya's engagement is interrupted by Lara taking public revenge on Komarovsky for her humiliation by him glowed as he watched Lara's protest, and he asks Komarovsky, 'What happens to a girl like that when you've finished with her?' Back comes the mocking answer: 'Interested? I give her to you!' Yuri reacts with the nearest we have seen to violence from him, snatching a cigar from Komarovsky's mouth, on the 'professional' grounds that he shouldn't smoke after a shock, and throwing it into the toilet. Knowing he has piqued Zhivago, Komarovsky twists the knife: 'I give her to you – as a wedding present.'

What follows is one of the film's most celebrated 'poetic' transitions and is worth considering in detail. As the door closes, church bells are heard, and the white of the toilet gives way to a dark rectangle. The image of a candle appears, and as the camera closes in, a face becomes legible through the condensation. Pasha lifts his hand to his glasses and Lara's face becomes visible to the left; she nods and then flinches as he seems on the verge of striking her. Our viewpoint changes to what could be his, with Lara gazing straight to camera, before turning to look out through the window and discover a sleigh passing, which carries Tonya and Yuri. He looks up, as if sensing the drama that lies behind the lighted window, and Tonya puts into words what she has realised: that he has seen the girl from the shooting somewhere before. He tries to deflect her by explaining that it was during a case and he's not supposed to talk about it, which annoys Tonya, and we return to the scene behind the upper window, with Pasha lying prostrate and trying to embrace Lara. The candle is still in the foreground and the bells continue to toll, giving the whole scene a sacramental quality, but even more striking is how these effects allow Lean to play this intimate exchange between Lara and Pasha without dialogue, as if in a scene from a silent melodrama such as Murnau's *Sunrise* (1927) (where an erring husband has to beg forgiveness from his wife).

The candle in the window was the work of Eddie Fowlie, using an ingenious arrangement of his own devising to make the condensation 'trickle down like tears' during the scene's long continuous take: 'I got hold of a hairdryer and fitted a copper tube to

the end like a long-barrelled rifle. I then placed boxes of dry ice with slots, through which I could slide false window panes sprayed with water.'[38] To achieve precisely the desired effect, 'each mark on the floor where the camera dolly was to be positioned had to coincide with the chosen size of the melting hole'.[39] Once again, this fulfilled what John Box described as Lean's aim throughout the film, 'to disclose rather than show'. But although the scene pivots on the candle image, seen from outside and within, it is also the inclusion of Yuri and his bride-to-be that adds dramatic poignancy. More than just Komarovsky and Zhivago's destinies are 'interwoven' in this highly compressed visualisation of the novel: Lara, Tonya and Pasha are equally implicated as the film traces its own web of fateful coincidence – as if Lean were consciously reviving the romantic fatalism of a Murnau or Ophuls. For a film made in the era of the 'new waves' that were appearing across European cinema, *Doctor Zhivago* resolutely turns its back on contemporary cynicism, or even the wry romanticism of the director's earlier *Brief Encounter* (1945) and *The Passionate Friends*. Yuri and Lara are indeed 'star-crossed lovers', who will achieve their short-lived union despite all obstacles.

'Your Country Needs You!'

The immediate obstacle appears to be Russia's entry into the Great War, although its chaos will in fact bring them together – at least in

The web of relationships: Lara seen with an anguished Pasha through a window lit by a sacramental candle, as if by the passing Yuri and Tonya the film. A dissolve from the attic room shows a priest sprinkling holy water over a military parade, with a brisk percussion-heavy march theme replacing the bells, which were perhaps intended to mark Russia's mobilisation. The novel contains no account of the beginning of the war, merely a 'cut' from Lara and Pasha leaving Moscow for Yuriatin to 'the second autumn of the war'. But Bolt and Lean felt obliged to provide the chronological framework that Pasternak had omitted, and the scene of a large celebratory parade is clearly addressed to western audiences who had recently experienced the fiftieth anniversary of the outbreak of the First World War. The method of adding a Russian flavour to the now-familiar spectacle of young men enthusiastically volunteering is far from historically authentic, but transposes the well-known British and American recruiting slogan and images of 'Your country needs you!' onto banners with Cyrillic lettering and a portrait of the Tsar.

Explaining how the war helped install Lenin's Bolsheviks in power falls to one of their number, Yevgraf. While his 'older' voice explains the Bolshevik view that since this was a war between rival imperialists, it didn't matter who won, a youthful Alec Guinness is seen following Party orders and enlisting 'to organise defeat'. The Gromeko family, including Yuri, watch the patriotic parade complacently from their balcony, representing the class that will soon have its world turned upside down as they enjoy their last

The iconic British First World War recruiting poster transposed to a Russian setting

opportunity to inspect the peasants and workers who make up the army. 'When their boots wear out, they'll be ready,' predicts Yevgraf. We see Pasha handing Lara their baby as he enlists, and Yuri at work in a hospital, while Yevgraf continues his cynical summary of the war's impact: 'Those who got back home at the price of an arm, or an eye or a leg, they were the lucky ones.'

As Lean and his team planned how they would portray the Great War's Eastern Front, revisionist views of the conflict were very much in the air – from Stanley Kubrick's powerful *Paths of Glory* (1957) and Alan Clark's influential book *The Donkeys* (1961), up to Losey's recent *King and Country*, with Tom Courtenay as a bewildered English soldier executed for desertion – and the muddy misery of the Western Front was invariably shown in sober black and white.[40] By the fiftieth anniversary of the war's outbreak, the callousness of officers needlessly sacrificing thousands of their men had largely replaced any sense of the First World War as heroic or patriotic.

The first image of a telescoped war sequence is starkly dramatic, with only the boot and hand of a frozen corpse sticking out of the snow in a desolate landscape (actually filmed in Finland). Overhead shots of trenches follow, with Yevgraf's commentary underlining how the soldiers were mostly led by officers they didn't trust. A gung-ho officer trying to inspire his troops is briskly contrasted with Pasha, shown fearlessly leading his men across no-man's land, accompanied by the rattle of machine-gun fire, before two massive explosions fill the screen, followed by a close-up of Pasha's spectacles without their owner. The image recalls a famous detail in the Odessa Steps sequence of Eisenstein's *Battleship Potemkin*, where a respectable older lady wearing glasses is seen bloodily wounded by the troops' vicious attack. But even if Lean had never seen *Potemkin*, as Brownlow asserts, it is quite possible he knew this widely reproduced image (which inspired Francis Bacon's painting 'Study for a Nurse in the Battleship Potemkin' in 1957). And irrespective of its associations, the image suggests that Pasha is radicalised by his front-line experiences, just as *Potemkin* – ostensibly commemorating the abortive 1905 Revolution – actually looked forward to 1917. Yevgraf's 'at last, they began to go home' is accompanied by another powerful close-up, of leggings emerging from a mud-filled trench and climbing out; then a mass of troops streaming towards the camera.

The 'beginning of the Revolution' is dramatised by showing two parties of troops heading towards each other on a road across a wide plain. Yuri's medical wagon is at the centre of the disorganised group, while the others are marching behind three officers on horseback. As they converge, the rebels try to persuade the marchers to desert, and one of the officers climbs onto a barrel to try to rally support for fighting the Germans, who threaten 'your wives and your country'. '*Your* country,' shouts a rebel, before the officer's speech is cut short when the barrel gives way, dropping him into freezing water. Another rebel casually shoots him, turning the water-filled barrel red as its top closes on the corpse. The slightly comic effect of this summary execution recalls another image which Lean would never have seen – in Eisenstein's first film, *The Strike* (1924), when the workers propel their tyrannical foreman into a river.[41] But then the Blimpish older officer is manhandled off his horse and brutally clubbed to death with rifle butts.

The now enlarged crowd of rebels disappears, and Yuri tries to help, calling to Lara – who fortuitously happens to be passing – to

An officer summarily executed recalls the anti-authoritarian rhetoric of Eisenstein's early films *The Strike* (1924) and *The Battleship Potemkin* (1926)

ask if she is a nurse. Their relationship starts to grow after Yuri admits he recognises her from the attempted revenge on Komarovsky at the Christmas party. Soon they are installed in a once palatial mansion which has been turned into a hospital now crowded with wounded soldiers. All we see of its exterior is a gate flanked by two statues of dogs, with other canine statues at the entrance. Perhaps it was a 'found' exterior in rural Spain, but in the novel this improvised hospital is set in 'the former residence of Countess Zhabrinskaya', in a small rural town which undergoes its own revolution during the months between the February deposing of the Tsar and the October coup that will bring the Bolsheviks to power. Bolt manages to distil the complexity of this account of the revolutionary upheavals of 1917 into a few easily graspable ideas: the Tsar has gone, and Lenin has arrived – albeit here reported to be in Moscow rather than Petrograd, which was then the Russian capital and site of the assault on the Winter Palace. The image of Lara accidentally burning her ironing as she and Yuri discuss their relationship is retained from Pasternak, although Tonya's offer in a letter to allow Yuri to pursue his obvious affection for Lara is omitted. They part, with no arrangement that they will meet again. The predominant colour of the whole hospital sequence has been grey, apart from a vase of yellow sunflowers which appears in later shots. As Yuri takes leave of Lara, two petals fall from the flowers, followed after a pause by

Yuri calls to Lara for help with treating the wounded, in one of both the novel and film's many coincidental meetings

another two. This further 'effect' by Eddie Fowlie may perhaps be an instance of over-egging the poignancy of this leave-taking.

Back in Moscow, Yuri encounters the world that is being changed by the war and the evolving revolution. The familiar view from the first floor of the Gromekos' house now reveals a shabby city, and when Yuri enters, he is met by a large crowd, following its subdivision into shared accommodation. He has to learn the new customs and language, under the disapproving glare of the house's superintendents, and discover how his now bereaved guardian Alexander and Tonya, and the son he hardly knows, have been coping with the privations caused by the Revolution. Apart from portraying the harshness and insincerity of the new regime (which disapproves of him speaking openly of typhus), the crux of this episode is a scene created by Bolt to link the narrator Yevgraf more directly with his half-brother. Yuri has been foraging for firewood at night and demolished a wooden fence, when he is spotted by the policeman. Perhaps because there is no direct contact in Pasternak between Yuri and Yevgraf, Bolt creates the convention that the latter is heard only in voiceover, summarising what he says to Yuri when he escorts him back to the house, where their apartment is being looted by the other occupants.

In the novel's much longer account of Moscow during 1917–18, Yuri eventually succumbs to typhus and becomes delirious; he later learns that Yevgraf has visited daily and brought them much-

Yuri and Lara's parting is mourned by petals falling from the sunflowers that light up the gloomy vacancy; yellow flowers will later announce their reunion

needed provisions. In the film, Yevgraf reveals his respect for his half-brother, without acknowledging him to be the 'better man'.

He surmises that neither Alexander nor Yuri realises the danger they are in (although Tonya does), and he urges them to leave Moscow before things get worse. Yuri's views are too independent, and his poems are 'not approved of', according to Yevgraf, who undertakes to obtain all the documents they need for a journey beyond the Urals which will take them out of harm's way. Along with hundreds of others, they gather at the station before dawn, where two rather incongruous giant posters present photographic portraits of Lenin and Trotsky, as if to stress that this is an early stage in the Revolution that will eventually expel Trotsky and bring Stalin to power; and they scramble onto a train which already carries forced-labour prisoners. The only one of these treated as an individual is the cynical Kostoyed, described in the novel as 'a grey-haired revolutionary who had been in all the penal settlements of the old regime and was now discovering those of the new'. Played with staring intensity by Klaus Kinski, he serves as a reminder of how ruthlessly the Bolsheviks were consolidating their grip on power.

As the train with its motley cargo of refugees reaches open country, it passes the smouldering ruins of a devastated village where a woman with a baby tries desperately to clamber on board, and nearly falls beneath the wheels. The actor in question, Lili Muráti,

The familiar view from the Gromekos' house, now communally occupied in a much-changed Moscow after the October Revolution

was supposed to grab Sharif's hand, but due to a misunderstanding, she fell and was injured, although not as badly as has sometimes been claimed.[42] What remains in the film is the take where she was injured, and the fact that Lean continued shooting with a double was held against him by some of the cast and crew.

Later, the train has to make way for another locomotive speeding past in the opposite direction, painted red and pulling an armoured carriage. This, we gather, is the mobile headquarters of the feared Strelnikov, who metes out summary punishment to opponents of the Revolution.[43] When we finally see him in close-up, it is clear that the former Pasha Antipov has become an avenging angel of the Revolution. Wandering away from the train, through a forest, Yuri suddenly comes across the all-red locomotive and is overpowered by its guards. The steely Strelnikov confesses that he used to admire Zhivago's poetry, although he 'wouldn't now'. He contemptuously dismisses Yuri's accusation that he had burned the wrong village – 'What does it matter, since the private life is dead?' Drawing the threads of the novel tighter, Bolt has Strelnikov realise that Yuri recognises him, and hear how they were both present at the Christmas party just six years ago. When Yuri refers to Lara, Strelnikov brusquely says that he hasn't seen her since the war but she is at Yuriatin. As Yuri is released, Lean inserts two shots of Strelnikov watching him leave, tightly framed by the armoured

Strelnikov's armoured train carries the born-again Red commander on his revolutionary mission, a possible reference to the trains that served as metaphors for the Revolution in Soviet cinema

window of the train. Having introduced the newly minted revolutionary by means of his red-painted locomotive (which recalls how often trains represented the impetus of revolution in early Soviet cinema), these valedictory images return us to the student Pasha, looking out as if from a prison at the free Zhivago, leaving to 'just live'.

'What a summer ... This is magic indeed'[44]
Zhivago was made at the height of the vogue for the 'roadshow' presentation of major films, which meant having an overture and intermission, or 'entr'acte' in this case, with music playing continuously over the image of an impressionist-style painting. This attempt to give cinemagoing the trappings of theatre attendance continued throughout the 1960s, and the format was applied to a wide range of different subjects, from the 1961 reissue of Walter Lang's *The King and I*, and of course Lean's *Lawrence of Arabia*, to *The Sound of Music* (Robert Wise, 1965), which would compete with *Zhivago* at the 1966 Academy Awards. In *Zhivago*, the entr'acte punctuates the long rail journey and coincides approximately with the novel's division into two parts. However, it ends with a rare modern re-creation of one of early film's favourite spectacles, the 'phantom ride',[45] with some fifty seconds of total darkness accompanied only by railway sound before daylight appears in the distance and the train carrying the camera emerges into a sunlit rural world.

A last glimpse of the ruthless Strelnikov watching Yuri leave recalls the former Pasha, seemingly envious of the poet's commitment to 'life'

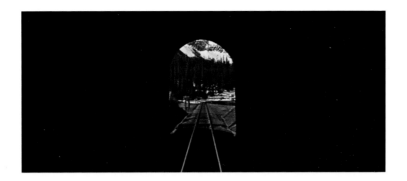

Eventually, the little family is deposited at an improbably picturesque Varykino Halt, where an aged coachman greets Alexander deferentially and offers to drive them to their destination. The country house at Varykino was built near Soria, in northern Spain. Its design was not finalised until relatively late in the film's production, when John Box found inspiration in an old Russian postage stamp discovered among set-dressing items. Both he and Lean were apparently seized by the image of this onion-domed structure, which was quickly planned and built. The building appears in two sequences, first when the family finds refuge, and later when Yuri brings Lara from Yuriatin for their winter idyll. Strangely, the original inspiration has never been identified, and as more than one commentator has noted, such onion domes are typical of Russian Orthodox churches, but hardly of country dachas.

With the main house barricaded by order of the local revolutionary committee, the travellers settle in an adjoining cottage for what Alexander predicts will be the happiest period of Yuri and Tonya's married life. Even news of the execution of the Tsar and his family, and of Strelnikov in Manchuria, seems distant. Their vegetable garden flourishes before winter snow piles up picturesquely around the cottage. But Yuri is clearly frustrated by the isolation and sits with pencil and paper, unable to write. The sound of Tonya ironing inevitably reminds him, and us, of Lara ironing at

A 'phantom ride' effect marks the end of the film's entr'acte and the Gromeko family's escape to Varykino

the hospital. Even as he reluctantly agrees to the suggestion that he visit the library in Yuriatin, the pattern of frost-flowers on the window turns from white to gold, and dissolves to a field of daffodils. The cottage is now surrounded by the yellow blooms – an effect that proved logistically complex to arrange, but is vital to the image-plot that will take Yuri out 'into spring' and lead him back to Lara. Two daffodils are seen in close-up, followed by the enlarged interior of one, which dissolves to reveal Lara's face lit by a pool of golden light. This was the image that I had reminded Julie Christie of; and it remains one of the most famous effects in the film, even if the industrial scale of daffodils required was mocked by those unimpressed by Lean and Box's unashamed romantic metaphor.

Lara is seated in the library and sees Yuri on an upper level.[46] He comes towards her, partly silhouetted, while she remains brightly lit. Their dialogue is minimal and banal, since it is the image and music that carry the emotion of the scene, and before long they are in Lara's apartment. Katya, her daughter, is at school, so there is nothing to stop them embracing and kissing passionately for the first time. Soon they are in bed, first indicated by a discreet movement of the covers, then seen talking in close-up. Yuri's return to the cottage is introduced by a track across the daffodils, before he is again seen in bed, this time with the pregnant Tonya. In Pasternak's novel, this period is one of moral torment for his protagonist, which reflects his own experience after

A first impression of the palatial dacha at Varykino, built in northern Spain to a design apparently adapted from a postage stamp

falling in love with Olga Ivinskaya in 1946 while remaining married to
his second wife. Since the film offers us no direct access to Yuri's
consciousness, it largely falls to Omar Sharif to convey this torment in
just two scenes each with Tonya and Lara. Geraldine Chaplin's Tonya is
essentially an innocent, although earlier, when reading the letter in
which Yuri refers to Lara as his nurse, she betrays a faint awareness of
his emotional attachment. But while they are at Varykino, she is eager
to please and excited by the approaching birth of their second child.
Yuri's growing attachment to Lara is deflected onto her daughter, who
appears during his second visit to Yuriatin and brightly reveals how her
schooling reflects the new values: in 'civic instruction', she has learned
that the Tsar was 'an enemy of the people'.

When Tonya asks Yuri to feel their unborn child kicking, he
decides that he must end his relationship with Lara, and invents an

'Magic indeed': Yuri is led as if by spring's flowering from Varykino to discover Lara
in a library in Yuriatin

excuse to ride into Yuriatin immediately. In an abrupt cut to her tearful face, she says, as she does in the novel, 'do as you think best'. His voice-off insists that this will be the end, as though to convince himself. We next see him immobile on his horse, as if still stunned by his decision, on a straight road through a forest. Suddenly other riders appear through the trees, and in one of the novel's boldest strokes – which also resolves its moral dilemma – Yuri is led off by Red partisans in need of a new medical officer. When he protests to the commander that he has a wife and child, a stern commissar played by the saturnine Peter Madden adds, 'and a mistress in Yuriatin'.

Capture and freedom

This abrupt intervention not only rescues Yuri from his dilemma, but sweeps him into the military action that has been conspicuously

Zhivago's moral dilemma echoes that of Pasternak: duty versus love, and guilt

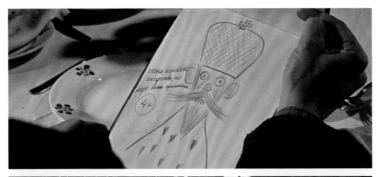

missing from *Zhivago* as an account of the early years of the
Revolution. But as with their treatment of the First World War, Bolt
and Lean are rigorous in selecting only what makes a necessary point.
Just two actual engagements are shown from the two years of service
that Zhivago endures. The first is a cavalry charge across a frozen
lake, in which the partisans seem to lose heavily against an
entrenched enemy. Shooting this on a real frozen lake in temperate
Spain would have been problematic, so it probably mattered little
that it was filmed during summer (although one of the promotional
documentaries about the making of the film reveals that this first
partisan engagement was shot by Nic Roeg before his dismissal).
Like the most famous 'battle on the ice' in cinema history, in
Eisenstein's *Alexander Nevsky* (1938), also shot during summer, this
involved preparing a level field to look like ice, which Eddie Fowlie

Encountering a new world: Lara's daughter is taught that the Tsar was 'an enemy of
the people'; and Yuri is captured by Red partisans in need of a medical officer

achieved by spreading cement over metal sheets, and adding many tons of crushed marble. One *trompe l'œil* detail completed the illusion (no doubt Box's contribution): a rowing boat is seen at the edge, cut off to appear stuck in the ice.

If unsuitable weather was a constant problem, so was the authenticity of costume. Brownlow relates how his friend Andrew Mollo, an expert on military uniforms, intervened to make the partisans' costume more authentic:

> I remember going out to the location and there were all these extraordinary figures on horseback … with sheepskins and shaggy fur hats. No swords, no weapons. But apparently my anxiety about these partisans had filtered through to David.[47]

When Lean asked what the problem was, Mollo was able to tell him that partisans at this time 'were mostly demobbed soldiers who wore army uniforms without badges', and that they fought with swords and rifles. Apparently, Lean had not asked for swords, 'because he didn't want it to look like the charge in *Lawrence*', an understandable anxiety, but both he and the costume department were happy to follow Mollo's advice.

The second partisan engagement reverses the balance of power, as we see their machine guns mow down a distant line of white-clad troops. When the partisans advance to inspect their easy success, the

The partisans' charge, like the battle on the ice in Eisenstein's *Alexander Nevsky* (1938), was filmed in high summer

enemy turns out to have consisted of young cadets, apparently led by
an older officer, whom the partisan commander roundly curses.
Yuri tries to help a wounded cadet, but too late to save him. This may
be a relic of the episode in the novel where he does succeed in saving
a young White casualty (whose mother's amulet had deflected the
bullet) by disguising him as a Red, but here it only serves to underline
the indiscriminate savagery of all civil wars.

We do not know how long Yuri has been serving with the
partisans (although the winter and summer engagements suggest
more than a year), but he has asked to be released. Although the
commander is openly sympathetic, the request is opposed by the
commissar, who insists on his greater authority, backed by the Party.
As the military struggle nears its close, he warns, the political struggle
intensifies, and 'all men will be judged politically', briskly concluding
the meeting. We might recall here that before working in cinema,
Robert Bolt had already made his reputation with a subtly dialectical
play about the struggle between Thomas More and Henry VIII, *A
Man for All Seasons*. Bolt's Zhivago is another man of conscience,
unwilling to bow to any ideology but also, we assume, haunted by
the relationships he has been so abruptly severed from.

As the partisans trek across a frozen countryside, they
encounter a group of women and children; the commissar asks one of
them who they are fleeing from: Red soldiers or White soldiers?

At a meeting conducted by the group's commissar, Yuri learns that he will not be
released from service, and that soon 'all men will be judged politically'

But the woman only knows they are soldiers, and we sense that Yuri has reached the end of his tether in this endless ebb and flow. He sees the sun show briefly through the gloom, and 'Lara's Theme' is heard as he turns round to leave the straggling partisan column. A dissolve reveals him riding alone far in the distance; and a fierce blast of wind shows him tramping through deep snow, with a long line of telegraph poles stretching to the horizon. The fake snow that had sufficed for many sequences in Spain was insufficient to convey Yuri's epic trek home, which was filmed in Finland, not far from the Russian border, with the telegraph poles that stake out his path a valued contribution by the art director Terence Marsh.

Eventually reaching Yuriatin, Yuri learns that 'the Moscow folk' have left Varykino, but he presses on through streets and alleys to the corner where Lara used to leave her key hidden behind a loose brick. The key is still there, now with a note of welcome, voiced by Lara. Stumbling into the apartment, he catches sight of his haggard, frost-covered face, which as we know was specially filmed by Freddie Young to simulate the effect of a breakdown.[48] In his delirium, he cries 'Tonya', but it is Lara who appears, and gives him a letter that has been sent to her for him. Abbreviated for the film, this explains that Tonya and her son and father are about to be deported to France, without knowing whether he may be allowed to follow. The film version does not include the information that Lara went to

Zhivago's long trek home had to be filmed in Finland to show realistic snowfields, with telegraph poles planted to give perspective

Varykino and helped at the birth of Tonya and Yuri's child, a daughter named Anna, but it does assure him that Lara is 'a good person'. Thus, Pasternak's theme of Tonya colluding in Yuri and Lara's affair, strongly present in the novel, is introduced into the film.

An unwelcome reminder of the past erupts into Yuri and Lara's reunion with the appearance of Komarovsky, who has survived the Revolution to become a 'useful' figure for the new government. He tries to persuade them to accept his protection and travel east on his special train, but Yuri bundles him ignominiously out of the apartment. The pair are now free to seek another kind of refuge, at Varykino. The music that accompanied the original drive to Varykino is now reprised in a joyful fast-moving version as Lara, Katya and Yuri approach the elaborate house the next day. Lara looks up apprehensively at the domes, but as they push open the door we are suddenly presented with the frozen interior in what is surely the film's most famous image, conventionally referred to as the 'ice palace'.

Nothing in Pasternak cued this revelation. In the novel, they arrive at dusk and 'burst in like robbers', so that Yuri 'never saw half the destruction; half the abomination' (p. 385). But for the film-makers, it became an opportunity to celebrate Yuri and Lara's epiphany, the brief winter of their undivided love. The interior was created entirely in the Madrid studio, and Box found his inspiration

Omar Sharif made up and shot to convey the rigour of his escape from the partisans

in pictures from the 1911 Scott Antarctic expedition, where snow
had blown into Scott's tent through a small hole and frosted the
whole interior. To achieve this effect on a large scale, Box and Fowlie
threw molten wax over the set and its furnishings, which was 'frozen'
with cold water and sprayed with mica to create an icy glitter.[49]
But what was Box's inspiration, apart from the texture of the

Lean and Box in front of the Varykino 'ice palace', whose exterior and interior have
become the film's most celebrated images

Antarctic photographs? The most likely source may have been from
his hero, John Bryan, designer of Lean's *Great Expectations* and one
of its most elaborate sets, Miss Havisham's room, unchanged since
she had been jilted on her wedding day. Like a benign version of Miss
Havisham's dusty mausoleum, the Varykino house is 'frozen in time',
but here its dramatic function is very different. As Yuri and Lara

Miss Havisham's cobwebbed room in *Great Expectations* (1946); back in the womb-like
place where he first learned to write, Yuri finds renewed inspiration for poetry

penetrate the house, passing through more semi-transparent doors, they reach the room with the dusty desk where Yuri's foster-mother taught him to write.

This will prove to be the Proustian key to unlocking Yuri's inspiration. Early the next morning, he rises and moves as if in a trance to the desk, takes out paper, pen and ink, and writes 'Lara' on a blank sheet. His writing, and later Lara's sleep, are disturbed by wolves baying outside, but essentially the idyll at Varykino provides the film's climactic evidence of Yuri as a 'working' poet, just as Bolt had promised. While he writes, Lara reads one of the poems and says, 'This isn't me, Yuri, it's you,' before he points to the title bearing her name. Clearly, this represents a major compromise on the part of Bolt and Lean. To present Zhivago as a poet whose chief inspiration is his love for Lara requires some closer identification than Pasternak provided in the twenty-five 'Zhivago's poems' that were appended to the novel, none of which makes any direct reference to the poet's love. Hence, the invention of a cycle of poems named after Lara, which eventually appear as a book with portraits of both Zhivago and Lara that Yevgraf can show to their daughter as a concrete, visible token of her parents. As with almost all films about poets or painters, we are shown the externals of the craft – in this case, Yuri's crumpled drafts – but never see or hear the words that are first censored, and then widely admired. Ten years later, Andrei Tarkovsky would include spoken poems by his father, Arseny, in his quasi-autobiographical film *The Mirror*, but that film was addressed primarily to a sophisticated Russian audience, not the worldwide popular audience of *Zhivago*.

The idyll at Varykino is cut short by a second visit from Komarovsky, this time accompanied by two guards. When both Yuri and Lara refuse to accept his offer of safe conduct, he persuades Zhivago that the recent death of Strelnikov/Antipov puts Lara in mortal danger, and so they appear ready to depart together next morning. But when the sledge will not accommodate all the passengers, Yuri says he will follow. As Lara disappears into the distance, he rushes through the frozen house to an upstairs window,

which he breaks to catch a final sight of her departure. The broken
pane, seen from outside, takes its place in a succession of framed
images through which characters contemplate their destiny.
In Komarovsky's carriage, Lara contemptuously tells him that she
knew Yuri would not follow and also that she is carrying their child.

Conclusion: 'the children of Russia's terrible years'

Pasternak's 'Conclusion' painted the 'last eight or ten years of
Zhivago's life' in drab and essentially realistic colours. He returns to
Moscow in the early 1920s, to experience the New Economic Policy,
described as 'the most false and ambiguous of all Soviet periods',
when Lenin introduced new freedoms to try to revive a faltering
economy after the civil war. He marries again, has two daughters and
dies of congenital heart disease. However, this is not the end of his
story, as an Epilogue carries it on beyond the Second World War,
when two veterans hear 'Tanya' tell her story of abandonment and
wandering, from which they are confident Yevgraf will rescue her.

It was from this final hint of redemption that Bolt created his
framing story of Yevgraf as the high Soviet official who wants to pay
tribute to his dead half-brother by finding his niece. After Lara and
Yuri have parted in Varykino, Yevgraf knits together the story of the
girl being lost in the Far East and Yuri's final years in Moscow.
We see him putting Yuri, dressed in a new suit, on the tram for his

As Lara leaves with Komarovsky, Yuri watches from another frosted window,
jaggedly broken this time to frame his last sight of her

first day back at the hospital. But from the tram, showing a more prosperous yet grey city, Yuri sees a woman walking briskly along the pavement who is clearly Lara. He tries desperately to reach the exit, but is prevented by the crowd of passengers and can only scratch desperately at the glass, in the final image of the 'window' series. When he finally manages to get off the tram, Lara has already disappeared and he collapses in the wide street, with a crowd forming around him.

At the funeral, Yevgraf marvels at the extent of Yuri's reputation and the numbers who came to pay tribute, 'even though nobody loves poetry like a Russian'; and Lara appears beside him, asking for his help to find her lost daughter. She is seen inspecting a line of children in an institution, while Yevgraf muses that although it was 'hopeless', he felt an attraction and 'was a little in love with her'. Lara's departure takes the form of a wide shot, apparently from Yevgraf's viewpoint, as she crosses a road bordered by a high black wall, where a giant poster of a smiling Stalin completes the series of portraits that began with the recruiting procession of 1914. Yevgraf's commentary catches the tone of contrition that had appeared in the USSR under Khrushchev: 'One day she went away and didn't come back. She died or vanished in a labour camp. A nameless number on a list that afterwards vanished. That was quite common in those days.'

Yuri's last, chance glimpse of Lara echoes their first encounter on a Moscow tram

Back in the framing story, Yevgraf is now much more a benevolent uncle trying to persuade his long-lost niece to acknowledge her parentage. Her young engineer fiancé calls to collect her from the interview and acknowledges Yevgraf's rank, although not deferentially. The location used for this framing sequence, the Aldeadávila Dam on the Douro River that separates Spain and Portugal, is now seen more fully. This massive structure, then the largest hydroelectric dam in Europe, had only been completed in 1963, and it is 'Russianised' by the addition of lettering on the outside of the control room, the beginning of which can be read as 'Stalin ...'. In the early 1930s, large dams such as the Dneprostroi on the Dnieper (now in Ukraine) were at the heart of Stalin's Five Year Plan to modernise Soviet industry, and a growing number of places

'One day she went away and didn't come back ... A nameless number on a list that afterwards vanished. That was quite common in those days'; a last link in the chain: the balalaika as evidence of 'the gift' of music

and institutions would bear his name. As the girl and her fiancé leave, the balalaika slung over her shoulder inspires an unashamedly sentimental exchange about her skill being 'a gift'. However, the closing image is of the great dam, a symbol of Stalin's industrial drive, with a rainbow – a somewhat hackneyed image that none the less echoes the final optimistic paragraphs of Pasternak's novel, completed during what turned out to be the short-lived Khrushchev 'Thaw': 'Although the enlightenment and liberation which had been expected to come after the war had not come with victory, a presage of freedom was in the air ... and it was their only historical meaning.'[50]

Finishing *Zhivago*

Filming ended on 7 October 1965, after 230 days. Brownlow records that many of the cast and crew felt emotional, with Lean himself saying, 'I don't want it to end.' This might seem surprising, after the catalogue of problems the production had faced during the past year. These included endless mismatches between the Spanish weather and the scenes due to be filmed: too much or too little sun, and never enough snow. There were also inevitable problems caused by the machinery of filming on such an epic scale and with such a large cast, many required to register in only a brief cameo. However, the lead actors had all proved to be troupers, with Omar

'Freedom in the air': Lean's final image amplifies the note of optimism that Pasternak cautiously sounded at the end of his novel

Sharif undergoing painful make-up procedures daily to appear 'Russian', and carrying on despite various injuries and exhaustion due to the gruelling schedule.

For Lean, it had been a relief to escape the interference of Sam Spiegel, which had marred both *The Bridge on the River Kwai* and *Lawrence of Arabia*. Ponti was an almost entirely absent producer, while Robert O'Brien of MGM was simply supportive at all crucial moments of decision. On location, the production manager John Palmer dealt with practical problems, having worked with Lean on three previous films, from *The Sound Barrier* to *Lawrence*, while Roy Walker, credited as an assistant art director, oversaw the large 'Moscow' set in Madrid. Eddie Fowlie carried on his role as Lean's leading 'dedicated maniac', endlessly on duty and willing to go to any length to meet his master's wishes.

Since *Lawrence*, John Box had become much more than head of the art department for Lean, and the gentle sparring between these two rested on a firm basis of mutual respect. Having first brought Lean to Spain, to shoot the Middle Eastern city sequences that *Lawrence* required, mostly in Seville, Box not only planned and designed the Madrid and Soria sets, but oversaw the choice of other locations for genuinely snowy exteriors. After Lean left for Los Angeles, to supervise the film's editing, Box remained in Madrid to design the titles, before being unexpectedly asked to join the director, who 'wanted to try things out on me'. Planning transitions between scenes had been an important part of their collaboration on *Lawrence*, as it would be on *Zhivago*, but now Box gained insight into Lean's mastery of editing. If a scene isn't working, he explained, 'we have to go back two minutes to find the rhythm'. Lean had asked Anne Coates, who won an Academy Award for *Lawrence*, to edit *Zhivago*, but she was pregnant at the time, and so Norman Savage, who had also worked on *Lawrence* (although uncredited), became the official editor.

As always, Lean was closely involved in the development of the film's music. Having won the battle with MGM to hire Maurice

Jarre, he originally hoped to use the traditional Russian balalaika theme he had played throughout the shoot. When the copyright for this could not be determined, Jarre was set the task of writing an equivalent, which he eventually succeeded in doing to Lean's satisfaction. This theme, associated with Yuri's love for Lara, recurs frequently through the film in different arrangements: notably when the lovers are parting at the wartime hospital, and again when the daffodils at Varykino foreshadow their meeting in Yuriatin. Later, it is prominent when Yuri escapes from the partisan unit, and when he is writing the 'Lara poems' at Varykino; and it returns at the end, setting the seal on Yevgraf's identification of his niece. The score was recorded by the MGM orchestra and conducted by Jarre, with the addition of over thirty balalaika players, recruited locally from among Russian emigrés, who were, however, apparently unable to read music. To Jarre's chagrin, much of the other, more varied, music that he had written for the film was discarded by Lean in favour of a repeated use of the Lara theme, which serves to link the central characters even though they spend much of the film apart.

The pressure to complete *Zhivago* in time to qualify for the 1966 Academy Awards was intense. Lean and Savage regularly worked until early in the morning, with Barbara Cole cooking at midnight in the bungalow of their hotel. Having been one of the most highly regarded editors in British cinema throughout the 1930s, Lean was apparently faster and more decisive in editing than on the set. He also brought in his own sound editor, Win Ryder, who had worked on all his films since the days of *Brief Encounter* and the Dickens adaptations. With the close collaboration of MGM's lab, Metrocolor, the film took shape as Lean had envisaged, although not as precisely as he wished – and the last of its then twenty reels, with a total running time of 197 minutes, was only flown to New York on the day of the premiere, 22 December. Lean would soon regret the haste with which this first version was completed.

3 Reception and Retrospect

Quite recently, I completed my chief and most important work, the only one I am not ashamed of and for which I answer with the utmost confidence, a novel in prose with a supplement in verse, *Doctor Zhivago*.

Boris Pasternak[51]

It's obvious ... that dystopia has completely replaced the love story and the antiheroic journey of redemption as the vehicle for our dreams.

Paul Mason, *Guardian* (18 May 2015)

Reception

The New York premiere of *Doctor Zhivago* at the Capitol Theatre has gone down in film history as a critical disaster, after the early edition newspaper reviews started to arrive and were, according to Lean, 'terrible'.[52] One of the first, and most dismissive, was Bosley Crowther in the *New York Times*, who began by stressing the film's length – 'three hours and seventeen minutes (not counting intermission time)' – and sarcastically mentioned the 'few rather major things' that provided the narrative's background, including the First World War and the Russian Revolution. He admitted that these are 'indicated in fine and fiercely acted scenes', before delivering the main judgment: 'But much the greater part of this picture ... is given over to sentimental contemplation of the emotional involvement and private sufferings of a small group of bourgeois who are brutally unsettled and disrupted by the circumstances of change.' Crowther's verdict could almost have been that of the official Soviet critics, who had condemned Pasternak's novel as 'slanderous',[53] despite the author's belief, expressed in his memoir *I Remember*, that it was his 'most important work'.[54] But the review's tone still seems surprising for Cold War America, even if Lara is described as 'the lost, estranged wife of a Communist' before the hammer blow comes: 'Mr Bolt has reduced the vast upheaval of the Russian Revolution to the banalities of a doomed romance.' In fact, Crowther's review strongly suggests he had never read the novel, which has little to say about either the First World War or the Revolution.

There would be no shortage of other US critics ready to praise the film, however, both in newspapers and the trade press: 'a monumental picture. A turbulent era is recreated in a vital, meaningful film. Transferred handsomely and eloquently to the screen, it is a masterpiece comparable to *Gone With the Wind*' (George Jackson, *Los Angeles Herald-Examiner*). 'One of the most meticulously designed and executed films since the advent of sound and color. Sweep and scope are captured by David Lean with soaring dramatic intensity' (*Daily Variety*). 'So big, it can't be ignored. Lean is one of the legendary great movie makers, perhaps the best around. It is as throat-catchingly magnificent as the screen could be. I could rave on and on' (Philip K. Scheuer, *Los Angeles Times*).

Big certainly, but for the heavyweight critics, it also seemed false and 'fustian', 'closer to Hollywood than to the steppes' (Crowther), with a 'method [that] is basically primitive, admired by the same sort of people who are delighted when a stage set has running water or a painted horse looks real enough to ride'. That verdict, by Pauline Kael, foreshadowed her later attack on *Ryan's Daughter* (1970) ('gush made respectable by millions of dollars tastefully wasted'), which would help drive Lean away from production for fourteen years.[55]

Similar verdicts would be recorded by serious critics elsewhere, as the film opened across the United States and Europe. And yet it has gone down in film history as a huge commercial success. The sheer box-office numbers seem impressive, boosted by the 'roadshow' strategy of the release, which limited the number of theatres and increased prices for those determined to see it early. As the official story reads today:

record breaking business in its second week at the Loew's Capitol Theatre in New York and the Paramount Theatre in Hollywood with both engagements having the largest advance sales of any Metro-Goldwyn-Mayer roadshow attraction in the history of the company ... second capacity week at the Loew's Capitol, January 5, with a smashing gross of $70,224 ... The second higher week reflected increased ticket prices for the New Year's Eve performance. With hundreds being turned away from the Loew's boxoffice during the first two weeks, advance sales in New York are now in excess of $200,000, and continuing to build. The first week gross of $35,877 at the Paramount Theatre was the biggest opening of any previous MGM roadshow attraction, topping *Ben-Hur* [1959] and *How the West Was Won* [1962] with first week grosses of $32,855 and $32,114, respectively. Advance sales in Los Angeles also are the largest for any MGM roadshow engagement.[56]

However, these numbers belie the reality, which was that first-week attendances were alarmingly low. But two decisive interventions transformed the film's fortunes and subsequent reputation. First, MGM undertook a concerted campaign to secure the success of their major investment, spending large amounts on advertising.[57]

New York premiere in 1965

In tandem with this, Lean and Savage returned to Los Angeles to re-cut and shorten the film, and re-record some of the music to fit, as O'Brien had promised they could.[58] According to Lean, there were no major deletions, but many small adjustments that resulted in an overall reduction of length:

If you ask me what I cut out, I find it hard to tell you, because there were ten seconds here and ten seconds there, getting people upstairs a little quicker, through doors quicker, and so forth ... There are no great lumps of film cut out.[59]

In effect, the first viewers had seen something closer to a pre-final cut than the considered work of a director who was also a master editor. And what the growing audiences saw, attracted by MGM's publicity campaign and the many favourable reviews, was the considered 180-minute version that was shipped out to the roadshow theatres and substituted at later premieres.

Despite the impression given by some stridently negative early responses, American critics as a whole were predominantly favourable, with the two heavyweight magazines, *Time* and *Life*, distinctly enthusiastic. *Time* hailed 'director David Lean's triumph over the challenge of filming Boris Pasternak's monumental bestseller', and Richard Schickel, writing a month later in *Life*, reflected on the mixed response:

[Lean] has received surprisingly harsh criticism from some reviewers, who apparently had hoped he would trump up some high adventure sequences like those that enlivened his two Academy Award winners [*Kwai* and *Lawrence*]. But Lean simply refuses to inflate his material for idle effect.[60]

Seemingly unaffected by its mixed notices, the film had a resounding success at the 1966 Academy Awards, held on 18 April in Santa Monica, and coincidentally the first of these ceremonies to be broadcast live throughout America in colour. Contending neck and neck with *The Sound of Music*, both films received ten nominations and won five awards – in the case of *Zhivago*, for Adapted Screenplay, Music, Art Direction, Cinematography and Costume Design, although Best Film and Best Director went to *The Sound of Music*, while Julie Christie won Best Actress for *Darling* rather than *Zhivago*.

Britain's turn to see *Zhivago* came in the wake of the Academy Awards, with a Royal Command performance on 26 April at the Empire Leicester Square, attended by Princess Margaret and her then husband Lord Snowdon, with most of the cast present (and proceeds from the charity event assigned, rather bizarrely, to the English-Speaking Union). Imprisoned for anti-nuclear protesting in 1961, Robert Bolt had been unable to get a visa for the American premiere or the Academy Awards, and wrote enthusiastically to Lean after seeing it for the first time:

It is a tremendously good film. Anyone who doesn't like it condemns himself. It's moving, powerful, beautiful, serious, and continuously held my rapt attention ... What's more, although it is always simply told and therefore intelligible, it is not in any way vulgar ... it isn't a trivialisation of the novel.

Bolt's confidence might also suggest self-congratulation, but the British reviews were, once again, mixed. Lean noted with satisfaction that both *The Times* and *Evening News* approved, although Alexander Walker (*Evening Standard*) and Kenneth Tynan (*Observer*) were unimpressed and took aim at Lean, suggesting he had become a mere photographer or a failed conductor of spectacle. Since *Zhivago* was not a British production, unlike *Lawrence*, and Lean was increasingly seen as a 'Hollywood' film-maker, there was no particular reason for British critics to feel supportive. The British Film Institute's *Monthly Film Bulletin* suggested charitably that it was 'an honest failure' in which 'the spirit of the novel has been lost', while *Sight & Sound* wearily attributed the failure to two long-standing traits in Lean's work:

Doctor Zhivago is a mixture of Lean's two well-tried methods of dealing with the classics: ornate Dickensian for scenes like the burial of Yuri's mother, or Yuri's own poetic inspiration by ice and candlelight; epic spectacular for ravages and battles and, of course, the long train journey from Moscow to the Urals ... The actors look good, but with the exception of Rod Steiger, who as Komarovsky has the most clearly defined role anyway, their performances lack momentum ... One is always conscious that nobody is Russian, and that nobody quite lives up to one's preconceived idea of the character that he or she portrays.[61]

Four years later, one of the new generation of British critics, Raymond Durgnat, would quote Lindsay Anderson's 1950 verdict on Lean that 'he had changed from the white hope of the English cinema to its white elephant', before praising Julie Christie's performance in *Zhivago* at Lean's expense, despite grudging admiration for the film's assured style:

To *Dr Zhivago*, an intelligent, rough hewn, Hollywood concoction, Julie Christie brings the rough, bitter, vigorous wind from the steppes of endured suffering, and a complexity which Lean seems to track rather than initiate. His perfect technique, delicate and strong, resembled a white statue awaiting a collaborator to breathe into it ardour and madness.[62]

In America, and indeed many other countries around the world, including Italy, where it played for a year, while leading critics often either disparaged or damned with equivocal praise, the public flocked to see *Zhivago*. The British Academy of Film and Television Arts may have given the film no awards, despite three nominations, but the estimated attendance in Britain was an impressive 11.2 million.[63] Since its initial release, there have been frequent reissues and a succession of releases on home-video formats, ensuring that the film has remained more or less permanently accessible for fifty years. And its reputation, along with that of Lean, has steadily risen.

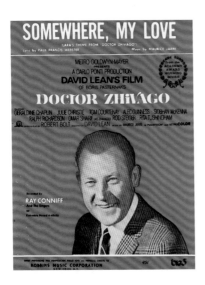

One aspect of the film's reception, however, has probably left a negative trace on its reputation. Lean's insistence on the frequent use of Jarre's 'Lara's Theme' undoubtedly played a large part in the tide of popularity. And when it was equipped with lyrics by Paul Webster, as 'Somewhere, My Love', it became an immediate success for both Connie Francis and, in a choral version, the Ray Conniff Singers. Foreign-language versions followed, carrying Jarre's simple waltz around the world in parallel with the film's release.[64] For many, it was clearly an essential part of the film's appeal, a forerunner of the omnipresent *Titanic* theme song by James Horner, although for some it emphasised, perhaps even suggested, the banality of the central romance. And as the music went on to lead an increasingly independent life as a staple of 'easy listening', it may have coloured the reputation of the film.[65] The larger issue of popular music and its symbiotic relationship with film, and with the field of 'light music', has yet to be adequately explored, but 'Lara's Theme' would undoubtedly repay closer attention for its groundbreaking role.[66] Several of the film's makers, notably John Box and Omar Sharif, felt that it ultimately cheapened the reputation of what they had done.

Retrospect

The worlds that produced *Doctor Zhivago* are all receding into history, almost beyond living recall. Boris Pasternak, old enough to have known Leo Tolstoy as a young man and to welcome the

Equipped with lyrics, 'Lara's Theme' became a hit for the Ray Conniff Singers as 'Somewhere, My Love' and has remained a staple of international popular music

Bolshevik revolution of 1917 that created the Soviet Union, lived on to see the first stage of Khrushchev's 'Thaw', after his denunciation of Stalin in 1956. But he died with his novel still firmly banned in the USSR, and Lean's film five years in the future. Khrushchev too had been ousted from power by the time the film appeared, and admitted to only reading the novel he had formerly denounced during his retirement.

Most of the film's creators reached their peak during the 1960s. David Lean had grown up in the silent era of film, and, although not allowed to visit cinemas by his strict Quaker mother, became first a respected editor during the 1930s, then one of the film-makers who benefited from the demand for British-made films during the Second World War to launch his career as a director. The designer John Box fought in the Second World War as a tank officer, then turned from architecture to production design and became one of Lean's closest collaborators, winning three of his four Academy Awards on the director's late films. Robert Bolt, whose second screenplay *Zhivago* was, had been a history teacher and part-time playwright, as well as a 1960s radical, before becoming Lean's chosen screenwriter for *Lawrence*, just as Omar Sharif had only acted in Egyptian films before co-starring in *Lawrence* and playing the lead in *Zhivago*. Three of the film's other leading actors, Julie Christie, Tom Courtenay and Rita Tushingham, were products of British cinema's 'new wave' of the early 1960s, before being suddenly transplanted into an imagined Russia that Lean and Box created in Spain.

When all these trajectories converged in the mid-1960s, they produced a film that now seems to belong to a different era of cinema – indeed seemed old-fashioned to many in the mid-1960s – yet remains very much a continuing part of our world, accessible through new media. In an era before CGI, Lean's avoidance of the traditional studio techniques of back-projection and matte painting actually aligned him more with his 'new wave' contemporaries, even though *Zhivago* was laboriously constructed and photographed in a variety of inauthentic 'real' settings. For Lean, it also marked a return to the stories of thwarted or misunderstood love that had launched his career in the mid-1940s, before its 'international' phase began. In this respect, its focus on the love story of Yuri and Lara is true to a central part of Pasternak's original intention. But the film's historical significance also becomes clearer in retrospect. It offered a panorama of Russia's history in the first half of the twentieth century that fitted with the prevailing climate of 'peaceful coexistence' introduced under Khrushchev's leadership, despite America's attempted invasion of Cuba and the Soviet-instigated Cuban missile crisis of 1962. Although shot mainly in Rome with an Anglo-American cast, King Vidor's 1956 film of *War and Peace* had brought the essence of Tolstoy's great novel set during the Napoleonic Wars to a worldwide audience.[67] Subsequently, one of that film's producers, Carlo Ponti, working with another Hollywood major, would bring Pasternak's chronicle of the Great War and imperial Russia's transformation into the Soviet Union to an even wider audience.

Henry Fonda and Audrey Hepburn in *War and Peace* (1956), filmed entirely in Italy

DOCTOR ZHIVAGO | 85

Today, the Soviet Union itself is already a disappearing memory, with Russia's citizens long free to read and watch *Doctor Zhivago* in all its versions. Since 1965, the novel has been adapted twice as a television miniseries, in Britain and in Russia, taking advantage of a format that allows for the inclusion of much more narrative detail.[68] And Lean's *Zhivago* has itself been subject to change, following the trend towards revised versions of films that began with Ridley Scott's 1992 'director's cut' of *Blade Runner* (1982). In the same year (twelve months after Lean's death), *Zhivago* was reissued in a 200-minute version, including all the material originally removed by the director in 1966; and other versions have run between 192 and 197 minutes.[69] No doubt this updating, as well as technical restoration, has helped Lean's *Zhivago* to retain a highly visible place in the collective memory of the twenty-first century, firmly established as 'a classic', and, like classics in all media, seemingly subject to shifting interpretations and perspectives.[70]

A more faithful screen adaptation? Yuri and Tonya's wedding breakfast in the 2002 miniseries adaptation directed by Giacomo Campiotti

Measuring impact in the internet era

There are indeed many ways in which films can achieve different kinds of cultural impact in the modern world, beyond what press reviews, awards and ticket sales could record in the 1960s. A study commissioned by the British Film Institute and the then UK Film Council in 2009 looked at a wider range of measures of impact.[71] These included factors like restoration, publication on home-use formats and the rise of internet-based quotation, reference and discussion – all of which, it was argued, could give films not only an extended 'life', but also an enhanced reputation. If we look at how *Zhivago* rates in terms of these measures, its immense popularity becomes even clearer. With over a hundred extracts and complete versions on YouTube alone, it has an average rating of 8.00/10 from 51,184 users of the IMDb site, but perhaps more significantly a total of 244 'user reviews' and nine pages of 'message board' queries and responses. Many of these are recent, dating from 2014 and 2015, indicating that the film is still being widely 'discovered' and vigorously discussed among admirers (and, it must be admitted, detractors).[72]

Nor is the legacy of *Zhivago* determined solely by the film's continuing accessibility. Cultural impact must include other ways in

Varykino reimagined in 'Lake Country, Naboo', the retreat of the Naberrie family in *Star Wars: Episode II – Attack of the Clones* (2002)

which it has become a part of contemporary culture. One of the most curious examples is how its original fictitious location – Varykino – has become a feature of the imagined topography of *Star Wars*, appearing in *Star Wars: Episode II – Attack of the Clones* (George Lucas, 2002). The *Wookiepedia* solemnly informs us that

Varykino, also known as the Lake Retreat, was the name of the island in a lake at the Lake Country of Naboo that consisted of the Naberrie family's retreat house. Generally, the name 'Varykino' was also applied to the villa itself. Convergence, the ancestral home of House Palpatine, was situated at some distance from Varykino.[73]

This re-fictionalised 'location', equipped with an extensive backstory, uses exteriors filmed at the Villa del Balbianello on Lake Como, with its interiors constructed in the studio, 'inspired by the basic architecture found in Caserta'. Why it is called Varykino may perhaps be traced back to the impact of Lean's *Zhivago* on the generation of the young George Lucas (b. 1944). Subsequently, Box's dacha design has been reproduced in virtual form as a 'property' for rental in the online virtual world *Second Life*.[74] Interestingly, the prospectus for this property weaves Pasternak back into his own fiction, noting that 'this particular Dacha was the property of the Author of Dr Zhivago, Boris Pasternak, near Yuriatin in Russia'. More broadly, it is clear that the interior of the Varykino house has become a reference point for fantastic or romantic decor. In 2013, Prince William and Princess Catherine were reported to be planning a lavish fund-raising charity dinner at Kensington Palace with 'a winter wonderland themed party inspired by the ice palace in the film Dr Zhivago'.[75]

A more immediate aspect of the film's cultural impact was its influence on fashion, already apparent in designers' collections from as early as 1966. Cinema has long interacted with fashion, setting new trends and amplifying existing ones, but such effects are often short-lived. However, the 'Zhivago look' continues to be a reference point, well summarised by the fashion blogger *Classiq*:

The costumes ..., designed by Phyllis Dalton, inspired a fashion revolution ... [Julie Christie's] beautiful and romantic wardrobe of fur coats, hats, white shirts and ribbon bow-tied hair styles ... [motivated] designers to use fur trimmed collar and cuffs on their winter coats again. Silk braiding and boots came back into fashion too. Marc Bohan, for his notable 1966 collection for Christian Dior, and Yves Saint Laurent were among the first designers to be influenced by the film's style.[76]

The same blogger also observes two more pervasive, and lasting, influences that can be traced back to *Zhivago*: military-style tailoring, which chimed with an ironic interest in military costume during the 1960s,[77] and oversize garments for women:

Almost all the coats and sweaters Lara dons are a size too big. She made the maxi coat a fashion must have overnight ... In 1967, *Time* magazine observed: 'What Julie Christie wears has more real impact on fashion than all of the clothes of the ten best-dressed women combined.'[78]

A promotional still (from a shot not in the film) shows the fashion dimension of *Zhivago* at its most persuasive (courtesy of Movie Ink. Amsterdam)

The worlds of *Zhivago*

Doctor Zhivago enjoyed some unusual conjunctural advantages: certainly the continuing echoes of the Nobel Prize scandal, but also the lingering effect of Khrushchev's highly visible appearances on the world stage, giving the USSR a more 'humanised' image than during the Stalin era, although it remained unknown to most foreigners. Paul McCartney would later say of his 1968 Beatles song 'Back in the USSR', 'it was a mystical land then'.[79] During the period of the film's production and release, widespread protests against the Vietnam War, and against other aspects of imperialism and late capitalism, created a new political awareness among large numbers of young people. Even if *Zhivago* was hardly seen as a militant, or even a political film, its portrayal of the origins of the Russian Revolution and the immediate aftermath was notably more sympathetic than had been common at the height of the Cold War in the 1950s, or in contemporary spy fiction.[80] Indeed, its failure to condemn the brutality of Stalin's regime, notably in the framing sequences voiced by Alec Guinness's Yevgraf, culminating in the appearance of an optimistic rainbow in the final image, led many to accuse it of undue sympathy for the USSR.[81]

But *Zhivago* also appeared as an unabashedly romantic story of self-denial and the brief ecstasy of happiness within a hostile world. And these are the qualities that echo through the 'long tail' of its discovery by successive generations of 'romantics'. New forms of realism were in vogue in the 1960s – Ken Loach and Tony Garnett's grimly affecting television drama *Cathy Come Home* was watched by a quarter of the British public in November 1966, before being reshown in January – and *Zhivago* manages to combine its romanticism with a palpable sense of the desperation that followed the Russian Revolution. The 'ice palace' interlude offers a magical temporary refuge in a world of constant danger and uncertainty; and perhaps the film's greatest achievement, combining design and direction, is its modulation from the opulent, hierarchical spaces of imperial Russia to the increasingly disorganised and precarious

spaces of the post-revolutionary era. Little wonder that its imaginary 'places' continue to attract the makers of virtual worlds, while its filmic qualities fascinate new generations of film-makers, such as Ewan McGregor, who expressed his admiration in a recent comment: 'It's like a master class in how to shoot and act and light … a lesson in filmmaking.'[82]

All films create 'worlds' that we inhabit for the duration of our viewing, although the language of conventional criticism often ignores the feeling of psychic, or somatic, immersion that this involves.[83] The very constructedness of the *Zhivago* world on screen, far from a 'true' representation of Russia or even a conventionally plausible narrative, manages to immerse its viewers in a complex web of relationships built around a central character who is, like most of us, essentially an observer. Through Zhivago's witness and empathy, we absorb the worlds created by all the film's makers, to emerge with the sense of optimism against all odds that Pasternak offered to his

Conflicting attitudes to romance: the grim realism of Ken Loach's *Cathy Come Home* (1966) on television's small screen accompanied *Zhivago*'s UK release in 1966 intended Russian readers. Like many of his generation of Russian artists, Pasternak believed that art was more important than mere life, and his novel, like his own life, bears witness to this philosophy of 'life creation' (*zhiznetvorchestvo*).[84] But despite an original poster that portrayed the romantic couple rising above the events that surround them, the film actually shows their story ending with remarkably realistic bleakness. A love story certainly, or rather an intersection of truncated love stories, and one that points 'beyond the stars'.[85]

Notes

1 Kevin Brownlow, *David Lean: A Biography* (London: Richard Cohen Books, 1996), p. 499.
2 The copy of the novel I have used for reference is the original 1958 edition, translated by Max Hayward and Manya Harari (London: Collins and Harvill Press) and already in its twelfth impression in 1959, which belonged to my wife's parents; a reminder of how widely popular it was immediately after appearing in translation.
3 Several accounts of this episode are summarised in Olga Ivinskaya's memoir, *A Captive of Time: My Years with Pasternak*, trans. May Hayward (London: Collins and Harvill Press, 1978), pp. 66–71.
4 Paolo Mancosu, *Inside the Zhivago Storm: The Editorial Adventures of Pasternak's Masterpiece* (Milan: Feltrinelli, 2013).
5 Peter Finn and Petra Couvée, *The Zhivago Affair: The Kremlin, the CIA, and the Battle over a Forbidden Book* (London: Harvill Secker, 2014).
6 Edmund Wilson, 'Doctor Zhivago', *The New Yorker*, 15 November 1958; see also Wilson, 'Legend and Symbol in *Doctor Zhivago*', *Encounter*, June 1959, pp. 5–15.
7 The only real competitor, Mikhail Sholokhov's four-volume *Quiet Flows the Don*, was first translated in the 1930s, and its strongly conformist author awarded the Nobel Prize in 1965, in what may seem a response to the Pasternak affair.
8 Robert Bolt obituary, by John Calder, *The Independent*, 23 February 1995.
9 A collection of letters to Barbara Cole, Lean's continuity assistant and confidante during the production of *Zhivago*, is held at the University of Reading, and was consulted by Brownlow.
10 Brownlow, *David Lean*, p. 500.
11 Bolt's wife Jo left with their children in November 1964, after which he went to Madrid.
12 Brownlow, *David Lean*, p. 532. According to Brownlow, Lean barely knew the Soviet film classics, which he thought had been excessively copied. His massacre sequence works mainly by showing Zhivago's mounting disbelief, with a bare minimum of stark details.
13 Ibid., p. 505.
14 Ibid., p. 501.
15 Ibid.
16 Bolt to Robert Stewart, quoted in ibid., p. 507.
17 *Moscow in Madrid* is the title of a four-minute promotional documentary about the making of the film, produced in 1965 by Thomas Craven Film Corporation.
18 Box, quoted in Ian Christie, *The Art of Film: John Box and Production Design* (London: Wallflower, 2008), p. 63.
19 Terence Marsh, interviewed in ibid., p. 64.
20 His role in *Zhivago* may have led to Courtenay playing the eponymous hero of Caspar Wrede's *One Day in the Life of Ivan Denisovich*, a 1970 Anglo-Norwegian film of Solzhenitsyn's 1962 novel.
21 Guinness, in a telegram from Munich, accepting the role, quoted in Brownlow, *David Lean*, p. 515. At the time, he was making a now forgotten comedy, *Situation Hopeless … But Not Serious* (Gottfried Reinhardt, 1965),

which may have encouraged him to return to working on something more substantial with Lean.

22 Brownlow, *David Lean*, p. 523.

23 Ibid., p. 521.

24 Eddie Fowlie and Richard Torné, *David Lean's Dedicated Maniac: Memoirs of a Film Specialist* (London: Austin Macauley Publishers, 2014), p. 176.

25 Freddie Young, *Seventy Light Years: A Life in the Movies*. An autobiography as told to Peter Busby (London: Faber, 1999), p. 106.

26 Ibid., p. 110.

27 Fowlie and Torné, *David Lean's Dedicated Maniac*, p. 182.

28 Brownlow, *David Lean*, p. 473.

29 Ibid., p. 537.

30 Brownlow records that Lean wrote out a quotation from Tolstoy after first reading *Doctor Zhivago*: 'The more a man devotes himself to beauty, the further he moves away from goodness.' Brownlow, *David Lean*, p. 519.

31 The film carefully avoids any precise dating of the frame story. In terms of narrative chronology, it should be the late 1930s, or the 40s as it is in the novel. However, on screen, the interview between Yevgraf and 'the girl' could be set in the 1950s.

32 *Zhivago*, p. 80. All quotations from the novel are from the original English edition, as used by Lean and Bolt. *My Sister, Life* was written on the eve of the 1917 revolutions, and became pivotal in the history of twentieth-century Russian poetry.

33 Phyllis Dalton, interviewed in Christie, *Art of Film*, p. 71.

34 Young, *Seventy Light Years*, p. 110.

35 Ibid.

36 Although always referred to as a 'rape', this scene has been the subject of considerable online discussion in recent years, much of it describing Lara's response as complicit. See, for instance, the blog *Game in Dr Zhivago*. Available at: <https://whyiamnot.wordpress.com /2011/03/09/game-in-doctor-zhivago/>.

37 Having Lara shoot Komarovsky rather than a politician, as in the novel, is an example of Bolt tightening the links between central characters, and sharpening the ambiguous relationship between Komarovsky and Lara.

38 Fowlie and Torné, *David Lean's Dedicated Maniac*, p. 178. This scene of Lara's extended confession to Pasha exists in the novel, where it is the night of their wedding during which 'his wounded imagination could not keep up with her revelations' (*Doctor Zhivago*, p. 95). The film's elaborate *mise en scène* might have been suggested by a conflation of two separate passages: first where 'Yuri noticed that a candle had melted a patch in the icy crust of one of the windows' (p. 81) as he and Tonya drive to the fateful Christmas party; and then the description of the intrusive light of a street lamp during the night of confession, which made Pasha feel 'as if they were being watched' (p. 95).

39 Fowlie and Torné, *David Lean's Dedicated Maniac*, p. 178.

40 Joan Littlewood's bitingly ironic production of *Oh, What a Lovely War!* (1963) broke many taboos about portraying the First World War and was filmed, in colour, by Richard Attenborough in 1969.

41 *The Strike* was not shown abroad until the late 1950s, during Khrushchev's 'Thaw', so remained unknown to Lean's generation. But apparently a major influence on his depiction of the war was King Vidor's *The Big Parade* (1926), several scenes of which are echoed in *Zhivago*.

42 It was reported that the Hungarian actor Lili Muráti (1914–2003) lost her leg after performing the stunt, but apparently she was back on set within three weeks.

43 In the novel's original translation, we learn that Strelnikov means 'the Shooter', and that he had been nicknamed Razstrelnikov 'the Executioner'; we also learn something of his background, as the son of a worker who had been imprisoned for taking part in the 1905 Revolution (*Doctor Zhivago*, p. 226). Mocking Zhivago, he tells him, 'these are apocalyptic times … a time for angels with flaming swords …, not for sympathisers and loyal doctors' (p. 227).

44 From a poem by the nineteenth-century poet Tyutchev, which, in the novel, Yuri writes in the diary he starts at Varykino (*Doctor Zhivago*, p. 252).

45 Phantom rides filmed from the front of locomotives in the United States and in Britain were popular attractions in the early 1900s, and even gave rise to a successful form of novelty film exhibition, 'Hale's Tours', where the audience sat in imitation carriages.

46 Pasternak's 'Yuriatin' has been identified as the city of Perm, on a tributary of the Volga River, which he came to know while working nearby in

1916, and apparently many of the locations detailed in the novel can be discovered there, including the library. A real 'Varykino', however, lies to the west of Moscow in the Smolensk region, far from the Urals.

47 Brownlow, *David Lean*, p. 523.

48 Young, *Seventy Light Years*, p. 110.

49 In his memoir, Fowlie acknowledges that it was 'John Box's idea', but insists that he 'executed it without any interference from the rest of the crew' (Fowlie and Torné, *David Lean's Dedicated Maniac*, p. 178). To which it might simply be said that all production designers depend on the work of art directors, set dressers and prop masters to realise their conceptions.

50 *Doctor Zhivago*, p. 463.

51 Pasternak, writing in 1957, the year before his death, in *I Remember: Sketch for an Autobiography*, trans. David Magarshack (Cambridge, MA: Harvard University Press, 1983), pp. 121–2.

52 Brownlow, *David Lean*, p. 538.

53 The largest public demonstration in Russia against Pasternak and his novel was on 29 October 1958, at the plenum of the Central Committee of the Young Communist League, when its head, Vladimir Semichastny, attacked Pasternak before an audience of 14,000, calling him 'a mangy sheep', who pandered to the enemies of the Soviet Union with 'his slanderous so-called work'. The language of this denunciation had been dictated by Khrushchev himself, it later transpired, who only read the novel after his enforced retirement. See Solomon Volkov, *The Magical Chorus: A History of*

Russian Culture from Tolstoy to Solzhenitsyn (Alfred Knopf, 2008), pp. 195–6; and William Taubman, Khrushchev: The Man, His Era (London: The Free Press, 2003), pp. 384–5.

54 Pasternak, I Remember, pp. 121–2.

55 Kael's original Zhivago review was in McCall's magazine, from which she was fired, before starting her more famous association with The New Yorker in 1967.

56 '"Doctor Zhivago" Opens to Record Breaking Business', 1966 MGM press release, transcribed by Brian Guckian (2015). Available at: <www.in70mm.com/news/2015/zhivago/index.htm>.

57 Originally budgeted at either $7 or $11 million (according to sources), the costs of the film had already risen to $14 million. It would go on to earn at least $111 million at the box office and has been rated among the top ten grossing films of all time (with due allowances for changing currency values).

58 Brownlow, David Lean, p. 359.

59 Interview with Lean, quoted by Gene D. Phillips, Beyond the Epic: The Films of David Lean (Lexington: University of Kentucky Press, 2006), pp. 355–6.

60 Life magazine, 24 January 1966.

61 Elizabeth Sussex, Sight & Sound, 1966.

62 Raymond Durgnat, A Mirror for England: British Movies from Austerity to Affluence (London: Faber, 1970), pp. 188, 190.

63 Julie Christie had won the BAFTA Best Actress for Darling in 1966. The main BAFTA awards in 1967, when Doctor Zhivago was nominated for Best Film, went to Who's Afraid of Virginia Woolf? and The Spy Who Came in from the Cold, while Rod Steiger was recognised as Best Foreign Actor for The Pawnbroker. The attendance estimate is from Ryan Gilbey, The Ultimate Film (London: BFI, 2005), p. 165.

64 By the end of 1967, MGM's soundtrack album had sold two million copies.

65 'Lara's Theme' as music, and as a widely used phrase in titling, has indeed expanded to an extraordinary extent. Try googling, and see note 71 below on 'cultural impact'.

66 The fact that Andy Williams included it on a hugely popular 1967 album, Born Free, along with other film 'themes', such as the title track and the Bacharach/David song 'Alfie', probably helped promote its entry into the repertoire of 'staples'.

67 Few if any reviews of Zhivago seem to have mentioned Vidor's comparable feat of selective adaptation just a decade earlier, or to have wondered if Bolt was influenced by the writer Bridget Boland's skilful filleting and compression of Tolstoy's massive novel.

68 In 2002, by Granada Television (226 minutes), and in 2006 by Central Partnership (416 minutes).

69 The current 'length' according to IMDb is between 193 and 197 minutes, but care should be taken with such declared timings, since different media formats can run at different speeds (television at 25 frames per second, for instance, rather than cinema's 24 fps). Nor is there likely to be any extant copy of the 'original' 180-minute release version which proved so popular. Comparisons between these multiple versions of many recent films has become a major branch of fan connoisseurship, with many blogs and websites devoted to evaluations. See, for instance, 'Director's Cut: 10 Theatrical Versions vs. the Filmmaker's Final Vision', *The Playlist*, 2 April 2014. Available at: <http://blogs.indiewire .com/theplaylist/comparing-10 -theatrical-releases-to-the-directors -cut-versions-20140402>.

70 See Frank Kermode, *The Classic* (Cambridge, MA: Harvard University Press, 1983).

71 For a discussion of 'cultural impact' and its application to British film since 1946, see Narval Media/Media Consulting Group/Birkbeck College, *Stories We Tell Ourselves: The Cultural Impact of UK Film, 1946–2006*, a study for the UK Film Council, June 2009. Available at: <http://www.bfi.org.uk /sites/bfi.org.uk/files/downloads /bfi-opening-our-eyes-stories-we-tell -ourselves-report-2006.pdf>.

72 A message board thread on IMDb headed 'Why is this film NOT considered one of the greatest films of all time?' has ten posts as of mid-July 2015, both positive and negative, and includes some sophisticated reflection on the film's long-term appeal.

73 Entry for Varykino in *Wookiepedia: The Star Wars Wiki*. Available at: <http://starwars.wikia.com/wiki /Varykino>.

74 'Ainee's fabulous new Ice Palace is a virtual copy of the famous magical ice-covered Dacha which Lara and Zhivago visit one winter. From the movie *Dr Zhivago* ... Decorated in lavish traditional Russian Aristocratic style for

you to furnish. Chandeliers, library, glowing stove and fireplaces all included. Open the stove doors to release glowing warmth when needed! Elegant Verandah is ornamented with sparkling icicles. Looks wonderful at Midnight too! Dachas were the summerhouses used by the Russian Aristocracy; they were often defensible, which is why this one has a tall look-out tower.' 'Doctor Zhivago's Varykino Dacha', *Second Life*. Available at: <https://marketplace.secondlife .com/p/DR-ZHIVAGOS-VARYKINO -DACHA-288-prims/478223>.

75 'William and Kate's New Court is Opened with £60,000 per Table Gala Dinner', *Daily Express*, 13 October 2013. Available at: <http://www.express .co.uk/comment/columnists/richard -palmer/435557/William-and-Kate-s -new-court-is-opened-with-60-000 -per-table-gala-dinner>.

76 'Style in Film: *Doctor Zhivago*', *Classiq* blog, 12 December 2013. Available at: <http://classiq.me/style-in-film-doctor -zhivago>.

77 The shop I Was Lord Kitchener's Valet, selling antique military uniforms to many pop musicians, opened in Portobello Road in 1966 and soon had branches elsewhere in London. The 1914 recruiting poster featuring Kitchener, which is reproduced in a pseudo-Russian version in *Zhivago*, was popularised by this fashion trend.

78 See an interview with the Bucharest-based *Classiq* blogger Ada in *This is Six: A Passion for Cloth*, 31 May 2015. Available at: <http://thisissixblog.com

/2015/03/31/interview-ada
-from-classiq/>.

79 Kevin O'Flynn, 'Paul McCartney
Finally Back in the U.S.S.R.', *The Moscow
Times*, 26 May 2003.

80 The second Bond film, *From Russia
with Love* (Terence Young, 1963), *The
Ipcress File* (Sidney Furie, 1965) and *The
Spy Who Came in from the Cold* (Martin
Ritt, 1965) all traded on continuing
Cold War suspicion of the Soviet
Union.

81 In a review of Richard Pevear and
Larissa Volokhonsky's new translation
of the novel, Michael Wood recalled
Kael's condemnation of the rainbow as
'disgraceful … a coarse gesture of
condescension and appeasement to the
Russians'. Michael Wood, 'Before They
Met', *London Review of Books* vol. 33 no. 4,
17 February 2011, pp. 9–11.

82 To which he adds: 'It makes me very
depressed watching it, because we don't
make films like that any more – and I
wish we did.' Ewan McGregor, 'Five
Favourite Films', *Rotten Tomatoes*,
9 March 2012. Available at: <http://
www.rottentomatoes.com/m
/salmon_fishing_in_the_yemen
/news/1924711/five_favorite_films_
with_ewan_mcgregor/>.

83 On film worlds, see Daniel Yacavone,
*Film Worlds: A Philosophical Aesthetics of
Cinema* (New York: Columbia University
Press, 2014). See also an interview with
Yacavone, *Columbia University Press Blog*,
14 January 2015. Available at:
<http://www.cupblog.org/?p=15620>.
On psychoanalytic approaches to filmic
experience, see inter alia, Andrea
Sabbadini, *Moving Images: Psychoanalytic
Reflections on Film* (London: Routledge,
2014), and Sabbadini, *Boundaries and
Bridges: Perspectives on Time and Space in
Psychoanalysis* (London: Karnac Books,
2014). Somatic theory is based on
hypotheses by the neuroscientist
Antonio Damasio, and developed by
others, including the drama theorist
Barbara Sellers-Young.

84 See Irina Paperno (ed.), *Creating Life:
The Aesthetic Utopia of Russian Modernism*
(Stanford, CA: Stanford University Press,
1994), p. 2.

85 A phrase chosen by Sergei Eisenstein
to evoke all that cinema could offer
'beyond the film stars', and used as the
title for the English translation of his
memoirs, *Beyond the Stars: The Memoirs of
Sergei Eisenstein*, ed. Richard Taylor,
trans. William Powell (London:
BFI/Seagull, 1995).

Credits

Doctor Zhivago
USA/UK/Italy 1965

Directed by
David Lean
Produced by
Carlo Ponti
Executive Producer
Arvid Griffen
Screenplay by
Robert Bolt, based on the
novel *Doctor Zhivago* by
Boris Leonidovich
Pasternak (translated by
Max Hayward and
Manya Harari,
New York, 1958)
Director of Photography
Freddie Young
Production Designer
John Box
Edited by
Norman Savage
Music by
Maurice Jarre

© MGM
Production Companies
Metro-Goldwyn-Mayer
Carlo Ponti
Cinematografica
Sostar S.A. (uncredited)
Production Supervisor
John Palmer
Production Managers
Agustin Pastor
Douglas Twiddy
2nd Unit Director
Roy Rossotti
Assistant Directors
Roy Stevens

Pedro Vidal
Michael Stevenson
Peter Beale
**2nd Unit Director of
Photography**
Desmond Dickinson
Camera Operators
Ernest Day
Manuel Berenguer
Stills
Ken Danvers
Special Effects
Eddie Fowlie
Art Director
Terence Marsh
Assistant Art Directors
Roy Walker
Ernest Archer
Bill Hutchinson
Gil Parrondo
Set Decoration
Dario Simoni
Construction
Fred Bennett
Gus Walker
Costume Design
Phyllis Dalton
Make-up
Mario van Riel
Hairstylists
Gracia de Rossi
Anna Christofani
Sound Recordist
Paddy Cunningham
Sound Editor
Winston Ryder
Film Laboratory
Metrocolor, Culver City,
CA

Uncredited
Cinematography
Nicolas Roeg
Matte Painter
Gerald Larn
**Continuity [Script
Supervisor]**
Barbara Cole
Technical Adviser
Andrew Mollo
Equine Consultant
Julián Benito Navarro
Assistant Editor
John Grover
**Supervising Sound
Editor**
A. W. Watkins

CAST
Omar Sharif
Yuri Zhivago
Julie Christie
Lara
Geraldine Chaplin
Tonya Gromeko
Rod Steiger
Viktor Komarovsky
Alec Guinness
Yevgraf Zhivago
Tom Courtenay
Pasha Antipov/Strelnikov
Siobhan McKenna
Anna Gromeko
Ralph Richardson
Alexander Gromeko
Adrienne Corri
Amelia
Rita Tushingham
the girl
Bernard Kay
the Bolshevik

Geoffrey Keen
Professor Kurt
Jeffrey Rockland
Sasha
Tarek Sharif
Yuri aged eight
Mercedes Ruiz
Tonya as a child
Klaus Kinski
Kostoyed
Gerard Tichy
Liberius
Noel Willman
Razin
Jack MacGowran
Petya
Mark Eden
engineer at dam

Erik Chitty
old soldier
Roger Maxwell
beef-faced colonel
Wolf Frees
Comrade Velkin,
delegate
Gwen Nelson
Comrade Kaprugina,
female janitor
Lili Muráti
train jumper
Peter Madden
political officer
with partisans

Filmed from late 1964 on location in Madrid, Soria and at CEA Studios, Spain; in Finland, Alberta, Canada; 35mm Eastmancolor (50T 5251). Panavision camera and anamorphic lenses. Three-channel stereo mix (Westrex recording).

US premiere on 22 December in 70mm Panavision blow-up, roadshow release 31 December 1965. Running time: 197 minutes; subsequently 180 minutes. UK premiere and release (70mm), 26 April 1966. Running time: 193 minutes; subsequently 180 minutes.

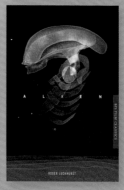